About the Author

Born in Poland during the soviet occupation, then raised in Canada. Worked as a chef for my professional life and made a lot of mistakes throughout my time on this earth that I learned from. Currently living in Alberta Canada with my wife and 3 children, and I am living life according to God's word.

Advice from a Guy Who Got it Wrong the First Time

Gregory Skolimowski

Advice from a Guy Who Got it Wrong the First Time

Olympia Publishers
London

www.olympiapublishers.com
OLYMPIA PAPERBACK EDITION

A CIP catalogue record for this title is
available from the British Library.

ISBN: 978-1-80439-944-6

The information in this book has been compiled by way of general
guidance only. Neither the author nor the publisher shall be liable or
responsible for any loss or damage allegedly arising from any
information or suggestion in this book. The names mentioned in this
book that are not public figures have been changed and/or nicknames
used. All personal stories told are to reflect what the author has
experienced, which may not be regarded the same by the other party
involved.

First Published in 2024

Olympia Publishers
Tallis House
2 Tallis Street
London
EC4Y 0AB

Printed in Great Britain

Dedication

I dedicate this book to my children, Sebastian, Gabriel, and Helena.

Copyright

A Brief History of Me - Why I am the way I am

I arrived in Canada in November of 1991, about 1 month before my 6th birthday. I am Polish by birth, same with my parents, and grandparents… and so on. My mother and father were the first to leave Poland in search of a better life for themselves and myself in the future they planned. Their story is not unique, but it helped shape them into who they became and what continued to happen in their lives, and mine by default.

My mother grew up poor, with a nurse for a mom and a drunk for a dad. They lived in a one-bedroom apartment in Warsaw all their lives. My mom did not have the best childhood as anyone who has an abusive father can attest to, but she tried hard for that not to bring down her spirits and ambitions for her future. She went to school five days a week from eight a.m. – five p.m. and had 9-12 subjects to study for per semester. Sounds normal so far (besides a large school load compared to what I had in Canada and especially lighter compared to kids in 2021 Covid Excluded).

What you know about Poland on paper from history is that it was under soviet control, communist/socialist, and poor. What is not understood is what it was like living under true tyranny. There were imposed curfews, tanks patrolling the streets, grocery shelves empty, and no food available for purchase. The people got tokens or coupons given to them by the government for rations and had to line up outside of grocery stores for hours to pick up their monthly allowance of flour, sugar, milk, eggs, and potatoes. People with young children got rations of formula. Sounds pretty good right? The government looks after your needs; In fact, the government looked after the people as well, and the typical monthly rations were only enough for most people to last two weeks. Regardless of your family size, you all received the same amount of food. Equality!

Regardless of the type of job you had, you were not able to take home more than a specific amount of money while the rest was taken as 'tax'. There were many Polish people working under the radar to avoid these situations of government theft. When you were caught and arrested, no one heard from you again. Do you think we have it bad right now when the biggest fight going on is about gender pronouns and nonsensical ideology? The time will come when you will find yourself without a place to sleep, without food to eat, without people to talk to... then you will truly know what to be thankful for and what life struggles are truly like.

My father was the 2nd of two boys to his parents. The 2nd boy of a mother who only wanted one. He was treated as excess luggage more than a human child. His father and he had a strong bond because his father was the one who wanted more children, but after realizing how his children were being treated by their mother, their relationship became unhealthy to raise a family in. My father struggled with his parents as time went on. His mother went to the USA to work abroad, and when she returned, she was more focused on how to handle her money than how to raise and take care of her children. I do not know much of my father's history because he and I did not have much of a relationship when I was growing up. He shared bits and pieces of his life with me, and it was painful for him to recall these memories. He became an auto-mechanic in Poland and was tuning up cars in the 1970s for fun. He ended up getting hit with a nightstick while protesting the Soviet communist government during the Cold War, and that required 2 surgeries on his collarbone, and a metal plate was needed to replace bone that was pulverized. As I grew older, I asked him about his giant scar, and that's when he told me about a 'car accident'. He only told me that he got in a car accident when he was younger, however, my mother set the record straight. It is possible that he lied about that part of his life because of shame, or because he wanted to shelter me from situations like that.

The conversations we had when I was young with him were not pleasant to recall, and he caused me a lot of grief. His father died in his mid-50s, and my father died in his late 40s, the day before my nineteenth birthday. I think that my relationship with him would have improved as an adult, but all I will ever have to go on was how he treated me and raised me... and it wasn't great.

My parents met each other in 1984, Got married in 1984, and had me about a year later. Their marriage was not smooth by any means. My father's mother did not want him to marry my mom because she was considered poor and if he went through with it, she would disown them. Even with the threats, they got married. Strangely enough, his mother offered them an invitation to Italy so they could go on their honeymoon, and my parents planned on using that as a means of escaping Poland and immigrating to Canada, the USA, Australia, or Norway from their honeymoon. They did not plan to return when they left. However, his mother lied about that and never gifted them the trip, which postponed my parents' plans to leave Poland in search of a better life. Soon after, I was born at the end of December 1985. Children always complicate plans, don't they?

After a year or so, my parents planned on leaving once again, but this time under the guise of going on vacation to Greece. They packed up all of their belongings and made the journey to another country. About halfway down to Greece from Poland in Romania, the front windshield broke on their car, and they needed to make the rest of the journey without a front windshield driving down the highways with me bundled up with blankets. When they arrived in Athens, it was about one a.m. They knew no one, they had no money, and no place to stay. As fate would have it, a Greek saw them struggling to find a place to stay and offered them lodging in his home for the night. My father sold the broken car the next day and both of my parents found a basement apartment to live in from that day forward.

Soon after both of my parents found work and aimed to save enough money to be able to afford the plane tickets to leave Greece for Canada. My earliest memory of Greece is when I was 4 years old (already living in Athens for two years) when I was going to school. I don't remember many details, but I do remember getting bullied in school. I was not able to speak Greek at this point, and it was hard for me to communicate with other kids and teachers. Not many Polish people had kids my age going to that school, but it was fortunate that we were able to meet other families that had the same plan when they left Poland. I remember a school made of white concrete with a large concrete schoolyard to play in. I remember sitting in the shade watching other kids play.

I was told that I was a terror to be looked after by every babysitter I had. I was a runner. It got to the point that my mom had to bring me to work with her because it was impossible to find someone to look after me for a few hours. So, when my mom went to work as a maid at multiple houses, I came along. I don't think that it is ideal for any parent to bring their kid to work, especially one that must touch everything, and has no concept of his surroundings. I almost walked off a double story balcony until the owner noticed me about to take a dive and caught me by my feet on the way off the balcony.

I would need a harness or a leash at the wet market because in Athens at that time, it was massive. You could walk around for half the day and still have not seen most of the booths and kiosks people had set up. So unfortunately for my parents, when it came time to go shopping, it was a borderline nightmare in waiting. I think in total, I got lost there… four times. Each time I was found with Greek people marveling at my hair and eye color and feeding me candy. Pretty good deal. They were amazed that I was able to speak Greek so well at this point, but my parents were beyond embarrassed when they tried to return all the things the shopkeepers gave me (like all of the candy). Polish people have a tough time accepting gifts because they think that by receiving a gift, you are indebted to the gift giver, and you must do something in return. It's a foolish way of thinking especially when that is never the gift giver's intention. How many presents or gifts have you given in your life that you expected something in return? If the answer is 1 or more, it's time to rethink the purpose of your 'generosity'.

Regardless, my parents did not accept any charity. It hardened them for better and worse. The better part was that they knew what they could achieve with their own 2 hands, but the downside is that they never went out of their way to help anyone in need. Both had difficult lives up until this point and it did not make things any easier when it came to showing trust in others. Many Greeks looked down on the Polish people that were coming down to try and start over because they were viewed as dirty people that are willing to take any job, and that meant screwing the locals of our work. Seems that sentiment is rampant everywhere wouldn't you agree? Regardless of the time and place, the "these people are here to take our jobs" mentality has and always will exist.

Eventually, we met another family with 2 boys and my parents became good friends with them. The boys were 4 and 6 years older than me so there wasn't much interest in playing together for them as they had other more mature interests they wanted to pursue. I can remember one story that was told to me when I was 4 years old going to school in Greece. I took my teacher's cup, filled it with water, and brought it to her. She looked surprised and happy that I would give her a drink. She drank a little, and then thought to herself that I was not tall enough to reach the water fountain... so where did I get the water from? Turns out, I led her to the bathroom and pointed at the toilet. I never thought anything of it, but my mom thought it was the funniest thing in the world. Even now she cracks up laughing trying to recall that story. There were other times my mom remembers about my childhood and the memories are not as fond. Namely all the times she missed anything of mine when I was little because of other obligations. My mom and dad did not attend any school event that I was part of as far as I can remember. I'm not sure how my father felt about that, but my mom was truly heartbroken when she remembered those times when she let me down.

To be clear, I did not, nor do I currently feel that way personally, because I was a shy kid, I felt embarrassed having people I knew especially my parents at school events. I didn't even want to be in these school events...

When we moved to Canada, I began attending school in

Guelph Ontario, and started in the grade One class. I did not speak a word of English, but I learned quickly. Kids always found it funny to teach me a swear word and then approach the teacher and say it. They all got a good laugh. The teachers on the other hand took me to the principal's office and called my mother. Another testament to the wisdom of teachers, thinking that a child with no English ability understands what swear words he is saying. So of course, the ones who taught me got away and I was sent to the office and put on a shit list. When I learned what the kids were saying about me, my parents, and immigrants, it made me a tad upset. I was always told in my Grade 1, 2, 3, 4, and 5 classes that I am not Canadian, so I should stop trying to pretend and go back to where I came from. Yes, even a white kid gets bullied like this, folks. Surprise! It's not just reserved for your token minority of the week. These are learned behaviors from none other than... their parents! And in part the educators since they see this happening and just stand and watch.

I ended up getting into a lot of fights. Enough that I had to bring a notebook home to my parents that had my behavior logged and for them to sign. So, whatever happened at school determined what type of punishment I received at home. I fought a lot as a youngster. Until about 1994 when I was in grade 4 when I moved to Cambridge, my parents told me that I had a clean start, and I should not fight anymore. That instruction slowly changed when my mom and dad realized how much I was getting picked on at school. I had cheaper clothes, I was bullied. I came from Poland and I was bullied. I did not have money to afford some extra snacks from the newly implemented snack cart. I was bullied. I got a hunchback of Notre Dame watch for my birthday, and a few days later one kid ripped it off my wrist because it was funny to bully me. I had enough at that point and beat the shit out of him. Then I got sent to the principal's office. My mom came down and listened to them explain to her what type of child I am at school and that I am continuously starting fights with the other kids. I got punished at home.

By grade 6, I was bullied so badly that I ran away from school during recess. I ran home crying, and I lived about 3km away. My shirt was ripped. I was bullied to the point that I feared going to school because it was overwhelming, and I had no one to talk to about it. My father worked night shifts, so I knew he was home. I don't remember the exact details of that day, but once I got home both my parents talked to me to find out what was happening. My father got so pissed off, he drove to the school with me, burst into the principal's office, and started ripping her a new asshole with his broken English mixed with a lot of Polish swearing which I had to translate at times. That was the last time I went to the principal's office. Funny enough the principal, who I will never forget, Mrs. H… told my father that I was just playing the victim and that I was instigating all of the fighting. She regretted saying that very quickly.

The bullying did not stop, but it was lessened enough for me to be able to tolerate it. There was always one kid named Mark that I would have the most issues with. He was very popular. He was also quick-witted. Oddly enough, I never fought with him, only with his idiot friends when they took things too far. Even he realized that at times.

I can remember one day at recess when we were playing basketball and some kids thought it's funny to throw the ball at my head. So, I confronted one of these kids whose name was Brad. As I walked closer to him, he closed his eyes, and sucker punched me in the mouth, causing my teeth to nearly go through my lip. I was bleeding heavily. He ran away very quickly, and I chased him. He ran inside the school to the principal's office because he knew what I was going to do to him. I went into the bathroom to spit out all the blood and rinse out my mouth, crying in the meantime. We both received a three-day suspension for this. It was amazing how you could suspend a child for being punched in the face... but hey, what do I know? Educators are heroes! From that day, Brad was telling people that he kicked my ass. Funny how that happens when some kids really take pride in their bullshit. Didn't your parents ever teach you that lying is bad?

I remember listening to one kid insult me because I was sweating on my upper lip. Next year I made that exact comment to him, and his response was "It's called puberty, Fag". He was right of course. That does happen when you hit puberty. You begin to sweat in really annoying places, such as your upper lip. It's amazing how kids cannot admit fault. It seems like this is a learned trait.

I remember my 5th and 6th Grade Teacher (was the same person for 2 years). I remember vividly what I had to put up with at a little catholic elementary school in Cambridge, Ontario; called Our Lady of Fatima. Mrs. W is what I will refer to her as. For what most kids remember she was a sweet woman who loved art. So much so that she would regularly have art classes instead of teaching kids the basics of Math and English because (in her paraphrased words) "I never really liked math or English, but I love art, and I think that teaching all of you young adults how to express yourselves is far more important". So as ten and eleven-year-olds... that's amazing! We don't have to do boring ass subjects like Math! or English! Yeah, it was great until you realized that our class was one of the dumbest bunch of kids in the city. We were taught about tolerance. Mrs. W loved to have kids express themselves with music, namely 90s grunge like Bush X, Smashing Pumpkins, and Nirvana. Rap and hip-hop made it into the mix too. Seems appropriate for a school setting with an 18+ maturity rating on most music, but what do I know? We listened to those bands for weeks on end. When there was one boy who tried to play dance music (me...) after three songs I was told that I had played enough, and it was time for other kids to have their opportunity. Yes. Let's listen to Mace and the one lyric "Why you on the wall hanging by your balls, lighten up Joe, no fighting in the club" was pretty much put on repeat because three kids found that to be the greatest thing they ever heard. Or even the South Park album with Chef on repeat singing "Suck on my chocolate salty baaaaalllls. Put'em in your mouth and suck'em! do do dodooo." Or the classic "Uncle Fucker". It was tolerated. What can I say? The funniest situation that I can think back on during my time there was doing a fun assignment and pairing up with a few other kids to do interviews about their future careers. I got paired up with the person I had the most issues with Mark. We worked well though surprisingly. He came up with the idea for me to interview him as the 'World's youngest Porn Star". As soon as those words left my mouth while we started our presentation, Mrs. W had to put a stop to it very quickly and write in our notebooks that we were misbehaving that day. She had the great idea of doing the notebook thing for bad behavior with 6 people in my class including me. I was a rotten child, apparently. I really did think of myself as a bad kid, but I can't ever remember doing bad things out of enjoyment.

Anyway, I can recall that she would be trying to persuade us to tell our parents that they should vote for the Liberal leader who was up in the next election because he would not hinder her art programs. You think your children are not being indoctrinated at school? Oh, hell yes, they are, you are just too dumb to notice. We were told by her repeatedly that Pierre Elliot Trudeau was THE greatest Prime Minister. Most kids had no concept of politics, so we just took her word for it. Turns out he was one of the worst our country ever had. However, because of all the kids taught by liberal teachers who were told this, who do you think went out to vote overwhelmingly for Justin Trudeau? The brainwashing starts early folks.

I sometimes try to recall any happy memories that I may have had during these years, but they are hard to come by.

I did have friends. I'm not sure what I would have considered a good friend at this age, but basically, anyone who did not bully me and was friendly was a nice change and I wanted to spend time with them. I was lucky that my neighbors during this time were a friendly bunch. It was a large family that lived across from me, and for the most part, they were great people... except their mom. She was... scary. She would clearly show favoritism with her kids and would be especially cruel to the oldest.

These kids could bring home a dead body and nothing would happen. The oldest would forget to take out the trash and he was grounded for a month. I tried to befriend them all, but I had the best report with the oldest Chris, and another brother with a very similar name to mine. Talking and playing with them, you knew that they had good hearts and were empathetic. The little sister was a little demon. Very rude, selfish, and obnoxious. It was ignored because she was mom's only precious little girl. There were seven children in total, and four adults that lived in the house together. Mom and Dad with five kids, one uncle with a daughter, and 1 aunt with a daughter. The dad and uncle got along well and worked together from what I can remember (possibly not, I never really asked). The mom treated the aunt like her personal servant. She was the one who tried her best to keep the house orderly while being used as a stepping stool by the mom. You could clearly see the difference in how both little girls were treated by the adults too. It was a sad situation now that I think about it, but I didn't think much about it back then because this family was for the most part kind to me (except the mom).

Long story short, the oldest brother Chris raped a girl and went to jail years later. At this point, the mom and dad sat down all the kids and told them that Chris was only their half-brother from their dad before mom and dad got together. That clearly explained why mom treated him like a bag of shit his entire life. Chris... I pray for you wherever you may be now, and I hope you atoned for your sin and were able to find some peace. you were a good person but lost your way. I know that years of torment can wear you down.

To be crystal clear, I do not wish harm on any of these individuals now, or even back then. I just wanted them to stop. Never did I hope and pray for them to die, or for harm to come to them. I always asked them to stop and just leave me alone. I became pretty good at being alone. So much so that now when I have a wife, two boys, and a little girl, it still is hard to comprehend that I have people in my life who love me and want to be around me. At times I find myself wanting to be alone even with a full house. It is really hard on your soul to deal with these types of situations growing up, and you realize what kind of impact they had on your life many years later; to the point where you just break down and cry for a few minutes reliving your past and coming to terms with yourself now, and how much you have grown. Pain from childhood is a very difficult thing to let go of. So many memories and experiences tie together to form the person that you are today.

Once I reached high school, things improved. I was not important enough to know, so I was not bullied anymore. It was blissful. I enjoyed my time in high school for the most part, but it still came with its share of heartache and disappointments. From girls that you like but don't know how to talk to, to friends that you made and threw under the bus, to just finding who you are and what you are supposed to be... High school is great. Just be mindful of the company you keep. Do not aim to be popular and sacrifice your morality or convictions because the cool kids are doing it. Do not fall under the pressure of smoking, or taking off your clothes, or destroying property. Those idiots just want to see you go down with them. Kids in high school already know where they are going in a way, and they can see themselves becoming a good person or someone gripped by evil, and the evil ones will always want to bring down as many with them as possible. Be strong and steadfast. Do not waiver. It is crucial. Oh, hell, you will make mistakes. Just learn from them for God's sake!

My home life was a bit different. When we came to Canada in 1991, it was during a recession. There were very few jobs available currently except for fast food. My mother took a job at Tim Horton's working the night shifts, and my father was unemployed at this time, trying to find work daily. He ended up delivering newspapers for a local publisher and ended up buying a worn-out Plymouth Reliant to do that job. If you can imagine the space and weight of 2000 newspapers, this car really handled itself quite well considering it was not designed to have over one thousand additional pounds of weight in the trunk. I often went with my father to deliver papers and I had a deal with my parents, that for every one-hundred papers I would run to the houses, I would get $1. Sometimes I got $2 for my effort, sometimes $5. It was a decent job to get my father by, but it was not enough to be able to support our family. I'm sure that he felt very inept because this was the case for nearly 3 years. It was difficult for my parents to survive on newspapers and Tim Horton's, but even though we lived very frugally and on government assistance for a few years, it was still a much better life than in Poland under Soviet rule. Granted, the Berlin Wall came down in 1988, but you can imagine that it was not an option to just give up and head back home. My parents had a plan and they wanted to make their new life in Canada, regardless of the adversity that would be faced, or the insults slung against them.

My mother had a goal of becoming a Hairstylist. When my father was finally able to get a factory job, it was night shifts, but the wage was now possible to support our small family enough so that my mother would be able to go to school to pursue her goal. The trouble with my mom is that she has goals and ambitions, but once she accomplishes them, she does not look for the next step in order to get better and her chosen field, she tends to look for a job that will pay more money, regardless of if it was her dream job or not. Throughout her time in Canada from 1991 until 2021, she has worked in fast food, in a hair salon, as a personal support worker in Long-term care, and as an underwriter in insurance. When she was in the salon, she did not look for greater opportunities to pursue, instead, she tried to get the most out of that one particular salon.

With her skills and experience, she would easily have been able to manage and own her own by now, however, that was no longer her ambition because of countless excuses she told us and herself. My father, Stepfather, and I all knew she would be able to do it because she truly does have the drive to succeed, however, it is almost as if she feared success. Office work is less stressful on the body compared to a PSW, but she found that job to be the most rewarding working with seniors. It was very difficult however because it was a property that had government assistance for funding, but it was poorly managed, and they were short-staffed almost every day. It came down to the point that being short 2 workers was pretty much standard, and the staff on shifts got used to the excess workload, but it became crippling when they were short an additional 1 or 2 people for the shifts. When people think that long-term care is nearly criminal now, you need to understand that it has been going on for DECADES. Staff have a quota to be able to deal with a resident for a total of seven-minutes, then move on to the next room. To put it into perspective, just filling out the paperwork correctly for each resident for their plans takes about five-six minutes. Now add lifting them, assisting with taking them to the bathroom, dressing them, and assisting with personal hygiene. It is an impossible task, and the majority of management will not lift a finger to assist.

Insurance was a lot less physically demanding, but it came with its own challenges. Sometimes you need to pick up the slack for a co-worker who does not file a policy correctly or does not bill the client correctly because the account was improperly set up. Imagine listening to some very rude individuals for 8 hours of your day, all the while mustering up all of your willpower not to lose your shit on them in return. Some people would call in and immediately begin to cuss out my mom, and all because they forgot to do something or provide something from their end. It can certainly become frustrating. Now she did extra courses and worked hard enough to not have to deal with customers directly, but instead, just look after policies. She is finally happy with her work and smiles far more often.

My father only had two major jobs here in Canada. One was the night shift for a few years at a steel factory, and then he ended up getting work at another factory in Guelph Ontario for the remainder of his life. He died on December 29, 2004, a day before my nineteenth birthday.

He and I never had a good relationship. He was cold, never gave praise, never said a nice word, and never spent time with me to just play catch, or even sit and talk. Any conversation we ever had was very one-sided, in that he would talk, and I would sit there with my mouth closed. If I opened my mouth, the conversations lasted longer and became more intense. That is not very pleasant when your father sits inches from your face and starts to talk. His breath was unbearable because he smoked, and I was more focused on when to take breaths instead of listening to what he was saying.

When my father was working night shifts, he was home during the day, and my mom worked afternoons at this time at the hair salon.

There were some intense situations I had with my father which I will leave out because I have made peace with it, and it will bring about pity for me, and that is not what I am looking for. My goal is to explain what my life was like to lead me to where I am now, and what things I needed to overcome to get there. Let's just say that physical abuse was part of it.

I stopped wanting to have a relationship with my father. I never spoke to him unless I needed to, I never spent any time with him unless necessary, and he never spoke of that day. Not once in his life did I have my father apologize for anything that he did to me. It was hard. All I thought to myself for years was that my life would be better if he would just die because then, he would leave me alone.

It is entirely possible that I could have mended our relationship if he was still alive, but it would have taken a lot of work. Years later it was still difficult to forgive him, simply because I could not talk to him to gain closure. The hardest task is to forgive. It is even more difficult to forgive something that happened in the past that can no longer be confronted. While it may be difficult, forgiveness is truly necessary for one's own heart so the process of healing can begin. I managed to forgive him in my heart a few years ago, and as difficult as it was, it was a necessary step to take to finally be able to make peace with my past and move on.

This leads me to the reason why I wanted to write this book. I have always wanted to help people, even if it be indirectly. Sometimes you have the perfect thing to say to someone who is dealing with tremendous pain but hold back because you do not know that person well enough and they might retaliate against you.

It has been quite the journey for me thus far, and there is still much more to go. Perhaps in 30 years I will finish another book and let you know how my own advice played out for me and my family. Thinking about writing another book before even finishing this one makes me want to quit now... but I must not! Even if you find that I am nuts, you will still have something you take away from reading my words. You need to know this. You will understand what it takes to finally come to terms with all that you are.

The Importance of Mindset

"It's not what you look at that matters, it's what you see." –
Henry David Thoreau

"Everyone thinks of changing the world, but no one thinks
of changing himself." – Leo Tolstoy

"You have power over your mind - not outside events.
Realize this, and you will find strength." – Marcus Aurelius

What is the point of even talking about this? To help rationalize
your thought process. Why do you think the way you do? All our
past experiences help shape our minds for the positive and
negative. Surprisingly, there is no way in our society to learn how
to think anymore, only what to think. Being constantly battered
with negative news or news of a specific context from sources
who all think the same daily will help influence you to keep
thinking negatively. If you are shown how awful and terrible
other people are of a specific race or political class for example,
this thinking will influence your actions without even taking the
time to ask yourself why.

Sometimes you learn the wisest lessons from those whom
you can only take lesser amounts of time with due to their
intensity or strong personality, to put it mildly. One big reason
we will not heed the lesson is because of the delivery. I can write
out exactly what to do to help improve your life, but in reality,
this will not be the right tool for the job, merely a guide to find

the right tool. Sometimes we learn the greatest lessons from those who have experienced great tragedy but have not been able to rationalize why certain things keep happening to them. Life can be very difficult for some, and very easy for others, but the main reason a person that has less than you is truly happy, is that they do not let the outside world influence their character anymore. Often those with more have less.

When it comes to the way you think, everything you perceive about yourself is the most important. Forget outside influence and focus on how you see yourself. Are you an alcoholic? Or are you simply a great person who has a problem with alcohol?

An acquaintance of mine put it to me this way when I was having a string of bad days: I AM is the most powerful statement you can make about yourself. I AM fat. I AM a loser. I AM not going to win. I AM not good at this. I AM too dependent. I AM a jerk. I AM…. "insert negativity here".

How you view yourself impacts how you actually think and behave tremendously.

It's funny to think about the saying "It takes 43 muscles to frown but only 17 to smile." It takes less, but maybe because the 17 are fighting the other 43. Those are some scary odds against the smile's favor! Think of it this way; There are 43 soldiers for the negative army and only 17 for the positive army. Negativity has a numbers advantage, but positivity has grit, determination, courage, and love. I would much rather have 17 good friends than 43 friends who are just there for their Instagram profiles.

Mindset is crucial to uncovering who you are truly meant to be. I AM a winner. I AM going to make it through this. I AM putting my faith in God. I AM never giving up. I AM always going to succeed.

There is a wonderful story I heard one of my Pastors talk about. He was going through an exceedingly difficult, if not the hardest time of his life. He was being berated on social media, kicked out of his own church, and losing many he thought were friends throughout turmoil that was caused by him speaking some hard truths. During this time in his life, he had friends of the family going through their own difficulties and needed to stay with his family for a short time because one of their daughters with spina bifida needed to go in for drastic surgery. He and his family gave prayers and support for the family visiting with them.

After the little girl had her surgery, Pastor Mark came to visit her at the hospital and asked her in that difficult time if she was doing well and would like to say a prayer. The little girl responded with a smile saying "Don't worry about me Pastor Mark, I'm doing great. Can I pray for you instead?"

Sometimes we realize how small our own problems are when we experience just the possibility of the burden of another. To what tremendous pain and fear the little girl is going through and her not even worrying about it, but in turn wanting healing and joy for him was inspiring.

The way we think about our problems creates the solutions.

Have a plan for the worst-case scenario but prepare for the best.

Collecting Opportunity

Let us start with the time you spend in high school and how it will shape your future. One great person I really enjoy listening to from time to time is Dan Bongino. He mentioned a phrase one day that really resonated with me, and it is something important to note. It is called "Collecting Opportunity".

He referenced the book by Nassim Nicholas Taleb called "The Black Swan". As mentioned, it is a book that addresses a lot of complicated issues, but one enlightening fact that it states is those that always succeed, whether they are good-looking or ugly, whether they are insanely smart or of average intelligence, whether they started poor or from a prominent family, they all have the same thing in common and that is they were collecting opportunity. They made their own luck. If there was an extra course that was offered and it was not required, they took it and collected that opportunity. If there was a lecture on a college campus after hours and no one else wanted to go, they went to collect that opportunity. They were invited out to a party but really did not feel like going because of one thing or another, they went anyway to collect that opportunity. It is entirely possible that they met someone special there that influenced their life in such a way it caused them to think more critically, or differently. They collected that opportunity. There is something that needs to be understood about this way of thinking. In every situation you get to participate in, there is always something you can learn. It is entirely possible that you might attend one hundred lectures and not learn much. It is also possible that you may attend one hundred and piece something together that could drastically change your life having listened to just 1 of them.

What this means is the willpower to be able to take advantage of every possible situation. For most, finding lectures to attend on topics they have no interest in is a very difficult thing to encourage. The idea behind this is to force yourself to take advantage of situations that you have no prior knowledge of or interest in, and by the off chance learn something new. Everything in life that we learn we can apply.

A fantastic way to collect opportunities is by volunteering at a retirement home residence, and Church. There are so many seniors who lived rich and incredible lives, and there are so many individuals at church that can help you with life questions. The ignorance of younger generations who believe that old people are just grouchy and boring farts who are just waiting out their final days are truly missing out on a world of knowledge. The same can be said of those who just think the church is full of a bunch of bible thumpers and Jesus lovers. While that may be true, if you have not come to terms with your own faith, perhaps it is an opportunity worth collecting. If you do not believe God exists, just ask yourself this:

Do you know everything? Unlikely. That's a No.

Do you know half of everything? probably not. No.

Let's assume you know half of everything. Is it possible that God exists in the half you do not know about?

You may talk to ten or twenty people before you realize who you have a connection with. You may find out something from their past that is relevant to your present and future. They are no longer concerned about what direction the culture is going, or what new social justice agenda is the hot topic of the day. Politics and Religion are distant seconds to Faith and Family. Learn from those who inspire you and collect every opportunity you can while you can. The older you get the less time you will be able to spend on situations that may prove to be valuable for you in the future compared to your obligations. I collected my opportunities by working on cruise ships for nearly five years. I learned about many different cultures and nations, and I became aware of what people truly value. I collected opportunities by going to a Christmas party from a job I was fired from, only to meet some unique people who helped change the course of my life. You will get some good advice in your life, and you will get a lot of terrible advice. Remember that the opportunities you collect are not always going to be beneficial or positive, but even the negative ones will shape you in a way that you will understand what not to do.

There is a time when everyone should realize that some advice comes from personal experience. What worked and what did not for that particular individual? Listen and learn. The advice might be incredible, but it could also be horrible. It is up to you to discern which you will absorb and which you will discard. As an example, there are several people who love to give relationship advice and never have successful relationships. It is probably not very wise to take the advice of a divorcee about relationships. Might be a better idea to listen to the couple that was married for 30 years. Listening to a salesman tell you what type of car is best for you is about as helpful as brushing your teeth with chocolate sauce. It may be delicious, but it will ruin your smile. Instead, speak to those who purchased the vehicles. Read forums and ask a mechanic about that specific car you have an interest in if it is prone to any issues down the road. The worst things I have seen are the women who have made terrible choices when it comes to their relationships, who then give advice to those who are in happy relationships. After experiencing pain, they tend to look inward and solely focus on what will benefit them or give them pleasure in the short term. Those are not opportunities worth collecting.

It may be a difficult feat to accomplish for the introvert, however, it is of vital importance. You do not need to go and talk. Just go wherever it is and listen for that opportunity to help improve your life by adding a little knowledge you didn't have prior. Collect every opportunity available to you.

There is another side to this. Dan references the point that Taleb makes in his book about chasing trains. If you make a commitment to be somewhere at six p.m., arrive at five fifty-five p.m. If you arrive late, the train will leave without you. If you arrive late, that's your fault. Admit when you screwed up and take ownership of that missed opportunity. It's a big world out there and it will continue to spin whether you're here or not, so take advantage of it and show up on time.

Goals and Ambitions

Goals are the object of a person's effort. It is an aim to achieve the desired result. An ambition is an ardent desire to achieve something through determination and hard work. Seems remarkably similar in fact. However, the perception of a goal is working towards a finish line with a desired outcome, whereas an ambition is much vaguer. You can be ambitious in your youth to become a sports star, but unless that is a goal you set, the ambition is equivalent to a wish list at the time of inception.

I have always been ambitious to write a book, but I never had a goal in mind. The goal of this book is to explain to the best of my ability how to be content in this life, and how to achieve your desired happiness without sacrificing any morals. Everything you need to know to be able to plan your life, to achieve your own goals, and to enjoy your journey until the end. Do not get me wrong, shit happens. I cannot say for certain that I will have all the answers in this book for those who grieve, struggle with depression, or are battling illnesses such as cancer, anxiety, fear, doubt, and anger… but I can point to those who can. My goal is not to change your life but to help you understand it and go through it with peace of mind and clarity.

To help you better understand where I am coming from and the purpose of writing this, let me give a quick rundown of my life until this point. I believe that it will help illustrate my reasons.

Wants and Needs

Wants are the things that we desire but are not necessary for our survival. They are typically things that we think would improve our quality of life or bring us pleasure and satisfaction. For example, someone might want a new car, a bigger house, or a fancy vacation. These desires are not essential to our existence, but they can certainly make life more enjoyable.

Wants can be influenced by a variety of factors, including societal expectations, advertising, and personal preferences. For example, a person might want to buy a luxury car because they believe it will impress others and signal their social status. Alternatively, someone might want to travel to a particular destination because it has personal meaning to them, or they believe it will be a fun and exciting experience.

While there is nothing inherently wrong with having wants, they can sometimes lead to negative outcomes. For example, if someone becomes obsessed with acquiring material possessions, they may neglect other important aspects of their life, such as relationships, personal growth, or spiritual well-being. Additionally, if someone spends all their time and resources pursuing their wants, they may neglect their financial health, leading to debt and financial stress.

What are Needs?

Needs, on the other hand, are the things that are essential for our survival and well-being. These are the things that we cannot live without, such as food, water, shelter, and clothing. Without these things, we would not be able to survive for long. Additionally, needs can include basic medical care, safety and security, and access to education.

Unlike wants, needs are not optional. They are fundamental requirements for human life, and they must be met for us to thrive. In many cases, needs are universal, meaning that they are essential for all people, regardless of culture, ethnicity, or socioeconomic status. For example, all people need access to clean water and nutritious food to survive and maintain good health.

However, needs can also be subjective, meaning that they can vary from person to person based on individual circumstances. For example, someone who lives in a cold climate may have a greater need for warm clothing and shelter than someone who lives in a warmer climate. Similarly, someone with a chronic medical condition may have a greater need for medical care and medication than someone who is healthy.

The Differences Between Wants and Needs

The differences between wants and needs are crucial, and understanding these differences is essential for living a fulfilling and healthy life. While wants are optional, needs are non-negotiable. This means that if we prioritize our wants over our needs, we may be putting our survival and well-being at risk.

Additionally, wants and needs have different impacts on our emotional and psychological well-being. Wants are typically associated with pleasure and satisfaction, while needs are associated with a sense of security and stability. For example, someone who has their basic needs met, such as food, shelter, and safety, is likely to feel more secure and stable in their life, even if they do not have all their wants met.

On the other hand, someone who is constantly chasing their wants may feel a sense of emptiness or dissatisfaction, even if they have a lot of material possessions or exciting experiences. This is because wants are often fleeting and temporary, and they can be quickly replaced by new desires. In contrast, needs are more stable and enduring, and they provide a foundation of safety and security that allows us to pursue our wants with greater confidence and peace of mind.

Another key difference between wants and needs is that wants are often a matter of personal preference and taste, while needs are more objective and universal. For example, someone might want a certain type of food or a particular style of clothing, but these preferences are not essential to their survival. In contrast, all people need access to basic nutrition and medical care to maintain good health and well-being.

Sins and Virtues

Imagine that you are a gardener tending to a plot of land. The plot represents your life, and you have the power to shape it through your actions. The soil represents your heart, which can either be fertile and receptive to growth or dry and hard, unable to support life. Now, let's say that sins are like weeds. They are the undesirable and harmful elements that sprout up in your garden, choking out the healthy plants and stunting their growth. Sins can take many forms, from the obvious, like stealing or lying, to the more subtle, like envy or pride.

On the other hand, virtues are like flowers. They are the beautiful and life-giving elements that you want to cultivate in your garden. Virtues can also take many forms, such as kindness, honesty, courage, and patience. When you cultivate virtues in your heart, you make the soil of your life more fertile, which allows the flowers to grow and flourish. However, just like in gardening, it takes effort and diligence to cultivate virtues and uproot sins. You must constantly tend to your garden, pulling out the weeds and nurturing the flowers. If you neglect your garden, the weeds will take over, and the flowers will wither and die.

So, in essence, sins and virtues are like the weeds and flowers of your life. You have the power to shape your life by cultivating virtues and uprooting sins, just as a gardener shapes a garden by tending to the soil and plants. By doing so, you can create a life that is beautiful, fruitful, and in harmony with your values.

The seven deadly sins are a list of vices that were first compiled by Christian theologians in the 4th century AD, and they are as follows:

1. Lust - an intense desire for physical pleasure or sexual gratification that is excessive and sinful.
2. Gluttony - the overindulgence and overconsumption of food, drink, or other physical pleasures to the point of excess.
3. Greed - an excessive desire for wealth or material possessions, which can lead to selfishness, exploitation, and even theft.
4. Sloth - a lack of motivation or initiative, coupled with an unwillingness to work or try to improve oneself or one's situation.
5. Wrath - uncontrolled anger, rage, or hostility that is often accompanied by a desire for revenge or retaliation.
6. Envy - a resentful feeling of discontent or covetousness that arises when one desires something that another person has, whether it be material possessions, social status, or personal qualities.
7. Pride - an excessive and unhealthy sense of self-importance or self-worth, often characterized by arrogance, vanity, or a sense of entitlement.

These vices were believed to be the root causes of many other sins and were particularly dangerous because they tended to lead people away from God and towards spiritual death. In contrast, the virtues that were their opposite were believed to be essential for a healthy and fulfilling life, as well as for spiritual growth and salvation.

The heavenly virtues are as follows:

1. Chastity - counteracts lust by promoting purity, self-control, and moderation in all areas of life.
2. Temperance - counteracts gluttony by encouraging self-restraint, moderation, and balance in all things.
3. Charity (or love) - counteracts greed by promoting generosity, kindness, and a spirit of selflessness towards others.
4. Diligence (or industry) - counteracts sloth by encouraging hard work, persistence, and a commitment to excellence in all endeavors.
5. Patience - counteracts wrath by promoting forbearance, self-control, and a calm, peaceful demeanor in the face of adversity.
6. Kindness (or humility) - counteracts envy by promoting contentment, gratitude, and a spirit of generosity and goodwill towards others.
7. Humility - counteracts pride by promoting modesty, selflessness, and a recognition of one's own limitations and weaknesses.

These virtues are seen as important for cultivating a well-rounded and virtuous character, as well as for avoiding the pitfalls of sin and the harm that can come from a lack of self-control, compassion, and humility.

The concepts of sins and virtues can have a significant impact on our daily lives and the generations that follow us. By understanding the nature of sin and its negative effects on ourselves and others, we can work to uproot harmful behaviors and cultivate a more virtuous character. This involves developing and practicing virtues such as courage, justice, charity, and humility, which can help us lead more fulfilling and meaningful lives, as well as contribute to the well-being of those around us.

The impact of our personal virtues and sins can also extend

beyond our own lives, as they can shape the attitudes and behaviors of future generations. By modeling virtuous behavior and passing on these values to our children and others in our communities, we can help create a better world for future generations. Conversely, if we fail to recognize and address the negative effects of sin in our own lives and the world around us, we risk perpetuating harmful patterns of behavior and leaving a negative legacy for those who come after us.

The choice to embrace virtue and eschew sin is a personal one, but it can have far-reaching implications for our own lives, the lives of those around us, and the generations that come after us. By striving to embody the virtues that counteract the seven deadly sins, we can help create a more just, compassionate, and fulfilling world for ourselves and for others.

How Politics and Religion have affected us in the last one hundred years

Both Politics and Religion have a purpose, but both have flaws. Both create laws for people to follow that may or may not make sense. Both have the best intentions of the people in mind, and both can be corrupt. Before I get carried away, let me explain that there is a right and wrong to everything. There is a right political ideology. Our spectrum right now is either Liberal or Conservative. Anyone who thinks there can be a happy medium is a fool plain and simple. There are times in history when one was needed above the other because without that push there would be no progress. The thought remains that progress is necessary.

There are timely ideologies and there are timeless ideologies. The timeless ones are what we hold true from the Ten Commandments. Unfamiliar with them? Let's break it down:

1. I am the Lord your God. Thou Shalt not worship any other but Me.
2. Thou Shalt not have idol worship
3. Thou shalt not take my name in vain
4. Remember the Sabbath Day, Keep it holy
5. Honor your Father and Mother
6. Thou Shalt not Murder

7. Thou shalt not steal
8. Thou shalt not bear false witness
9. Thou shalt not commit adultery
10. Thou shalt not covet

Those are the original commandments; any others have been edited for each specific religion that needed them changed to be relative and convenient. Catholics for example remove the 2nd commandment of Idol worship and instead split the 10th to not coveting your neighbor's wife, and not coveting your neighbor's possessions. Why may you ask? Because the entire religion is based on Idol worship. Jesus on the Cross as your symbol is idol worship. Mary, the saints, the Pope, and the entire clergy are designed as a form of Idol worship.

In culture, there are other idols that many worship, and the majority of them are celebrities and sports stars. Removing a commandment makes it permissible in the religion to do as you please in that regard. Perhaps too many of us worship our bank accounts, our sports teams, or our spouses or children. Why do I bring this up? simple. Conservatives want to preserve the laws of God; Liberals want to edit the rules to suit their needs. Everything that is downstream of culture and politics is based on moral or immoral behaviors we want to feel good about.

The main difference between a Liberal and a Conservative is their thought process. Liberals want freedom from consequences, Conservatives want to preserve the way of life they grow up with. The unfortunate truth in this case is that while we push forward with Liberal policies, even when Conservatives attain and retain political power, they cave too easily to the feel-good politics of Liberals and in turn, become slightly more liberal themselves. The reality is that most conservatives are very cowardly when it comes to social policy. Because there are many types of conservatives and many types of ideas that want to be conveyed, conservatives are rarely united on all fronts to be able to push back a liberal agenda. Liberals are exceptionally good at putting petty differences aside to drive their key arguments home. While this looks beneficial for liberals, the ideas that are being championed are rarely in the greater interest of self-preservation and moral ideology. Let's go through the major liberal points that have been pushed forward in the last one hundred years that have gotten very cowardly opposition by starting off with the big one:

Abortion.

Since ancient Greece, Hippocrates, Aristotle, and Plato, abortion was encouraged by the Greeks as a way of curbing population. Hippocrates advised that the best way for ancient Greeks to try and abort a child was through violent exercise. Aristotle and Plato advocated abortion because they saw it as more important to keep an economically healthy state.

According to Collier's Encyclopedia in 1991 (yes thirty-years ago), the estimated rate of abortions was 30-55 million per year and climbing. Many liberalized countries in Europe including the United States advocated the wider availability of abortion starting in 1965. The reason was to curb population growth. Seems like a popular reason…

Presently, abortion is a widely available procedure in the majority of Western nations, and now it is used to champion women's rights. "My body my choice" is the popular slogan used.

In the United States, the Democrats were the ones to push

forward with these policies and cite that women's rights are hanging in the balance when a rape victim or a victim of incest cannot be helped by removing the unborn child. These incidents currently are about 0.1 percent of the reasons why children are aborted according to Planned Parenthood. The greatest reason why women get abortions is simply two things: They do not want their lives altered, and/or they cannot afford to raise a child.

According to the CDC and Planned Parenthood in the US from 1978 - 2018, there were 186 abortions performed for every 1000 births. By this logic, about 18 percent of women who get pregnant in the United States will have or have had an abortion. The rate of adoption options offered and chosen compared to abortions is 1 in 133. That means one woman will choose to give birth to their child and give it up for adoption compared to one hundred and thirty-three women who will go through with an abortion instead. As far as racial background goes, white women (of any nationality) are 38.7 percent of all total abortions. Black women account for 33.6 percent, and Hispanic account for 20 percent.

Let's look at this for a second. The total number of Black people living in the US makes up about 14 percent of the country's total population. For argument's sake, let's say it is evenly divided between men and women, meaning that there are 7 percent black men, and 7 percent black women in the country. This means that 7 percent of black women account for 33.6 percent of the total abortions in the country as of 2019. Why is it so ridiculously high among black women you ask? Margaret Sanger. She is the founder of Planned Parenthood, and a very vocal racist and eugenicist for her time, pushing for eugenics of inferior races (in her point of view), and encouraging women of color to have abortions in poor communities by convincing them that it is the responsible thing to do if you cannot afford to raise a child. The reason that Planned Parenthood has made its mark on the black community most of all is because of this woman. And the Democrat party. Statistically, the poorest and most rundown neighborhoods in the United States have been Democrat-run for decades, and they also have the highest concentration of abortion clinics per capita in black urban neighborhoods in major cities.

The big trial of the century in the US was Roe vs. Wade. Long story short, Roe alleged that she was unmarried and pregnant and that she wished to terminate her pregnancy with an abortion performed by a competent, licensed physician, under safe, clinical conditions. The trouble was that because she lived in Texas and the only right to abortion in that state at that time was only if you were the victim of rape, or her life was in no immediate danger due to her pregnancy, the state did not allow for her to receive said procedure. She could not afford to travel to another jurisdiction in order to secure a legal abortion under safe conditions. Her Lawyers claimed that the Texas statutes were unconstitutionally vague and that they abridged her right to personal privacy, protected by the First, Fourth, Fifth, Ninth, and Fourteenth Amendments. By an amendment to her complaint Roe purported to sue 'on behalf of herself and all other women similarly situated. Needless to say, she won the case. What you do not hear is that a few years later she regretted the decisions she made making the court case and the choice she wanted to make to end her child's life. From what I understand she did not even go through with the abortion. She became a practicing Christian with remorse for her actions.

Well, that's fine and all, but I think it is very important to know the story of the founder of Planned Parenthood and why people of color are disproportionately targeted for these services in the name of women's health.

Margaret Sanger was born in 1879, being one of eleven children. Mother was a Catholic, her Father was an Atheist. her mother died at an early age and experienced multiple miscarriages. Her mother's cause of death was listed as tuberculosis, but she believed that her body became weak from birthing so many children and having so many miscarriages. This created a deep-seated disdain for large families and created the belief that women should be limited in the number of children they are allowed to have.

She went to nursing school but did not finish. She married and had three children. Although she did not finish nursing school, she worked in a poor immigrant section of New York City as a nurse, where she began to advocate and teach the importance of birth control.

Then in 1914, she started her own publication which advocated for women using birth control. She mailed out this publication. Doing so caused her to be in violation of the Comstock Act, which made it illegal to circulate unethical writing through the mail. She ended up facing possible jail time for her actions, so she fled to England where she could continue to do her research without those pesky limitations of morality the US had in place with their laws.

A Year later the US dropped charges against her, and she moved back to the United States, and shortly after opened the first birth control clinic. A little over a week later, she was arrested and spent 30 days in jail for violating the same Comstock Act. She appealed the charges, but they were struck down, however, the judge in the case did make an exception to the law that would allow doctors to prescribe birth control for medical reasons. This opened the door for the future legalization of contraceptives.

In 1917, Sanger began to publish and edit "The Birth Control Review", which was edited by her until 1929. In 1921, she founded the American Birth Control League, which later became Planned Parenthood. She really loved advocating for contraceptives and also advocated and spread eugenics as part of her birth control mentality, citing many through letters that the ultimate goal was to eliminate unwanted people. One such quote read as follows:

"We do not want word to go out that we want to exterminate the Negro population and the minister is the man who can straighten out that idea if it ever occurs to any of their more rebellious members." ~ *Letter from Margaret Sanger to Dr. C.J. Gamble.*

December 10th, 1939

Another, published in her founding publication:

"On the other hand, the mass of ignorant Negroes still breed carelessly and disastrously, so that the increase among Negroes, even more than the increase among whites, is from that part of the population least intelligent and fit, and least able to rear their children properly."

~W.E.B. DuBois, Professor of Sociology, Atlanta University. "Black Folk and Birth Control." Birth Control Review, Volume XXII, Number 8 (New Series, May 1938, the "Negro Number"), page 90.

Another:

"In the early history of the race... The weak died early or were killed. Today, however, civilization has brought sympathy, pity, tenderness and other lofty and worthy sentiments, which interfere with the law of natural selection. We are now in a state where our charities, our compensation acts, our pensions, hospitals and even our drainage and sanitary equipment all tend to keep alive the sickly and weak, who are allowed to propagate and in turn produce a race of degenerates".

~Margaret Sanger. "Birth Control and Women's Health." (Birth Control Review, Volume I, Number 12 [December 1917], page 7.)

She continues; In "Birth Control and Racial Betterment," Sanger writes:

"We who advocate birth control, on the other hand, lay all our emphasis upon stopping not only the reproduction of the unfit but upon stopping all reproduction when there is not economic means of providing proper care for those who are born in health."

Brian Clowes, PhD, was the director of education and research at HLI (Center for Heart and Lung Innovation) who had the pleasure of reading all 5,631 pages of the "Birth Control Review", he wrote:

Sanger was associated with racists and anti-Semites, people

50

who despised everyone who was not a Nordic god or goddess, and those who demanded coercive eugenics programs to eliminate 'lesser' humans. The whole bunch, of course, participated in continuous vicious attacks on the Catholic Church.... The malignant influence of Sanger and similar thinkers not only has ruined the West to the point that it is dying, but seems hell-bent on corrupting the rest of the world as well."

Clowes' massive library compiled at HLI contains thousands of texts, including many of Sanger's writings. He went on to say:

"The Birth Control Review frequently highlighted the mission of its parent organization: 'The American Birth Control League'. Its Aim: To promote eugenic birth selection throughout the United States so that there may be more well-born and fewer ill-born children—a stronger, healthier and more intelligent race."

We witnessed the eugenic philosophy enacted during World War II in the extermination of six million Jews not too long after Sanger was advocating for her movement, which gained a lot of Nazi support in the 1930s. Margaret Sanger gave evidence many times over in her correlation of birth control and eugenics through her writings and speeches. As the author of articles entitled "The Eugenic Value of Birth Control Propaganda" and "Birth Control and Racial Betterment", Margaret showed the world her true intentions and the underlying reasons why she thought the world needed birth control, but sadly in a lot of popular publications in the modern day, these are very difficult facts to find as they are all becoming suppressed because there is a narrative being pushed.

Fun fact: William Moulton Marston, who was a famous psychologist, made up Wonder Woman in 1941. He was interested in the women's suffrage movement and in Margaret Sanger, the birth control and women's rights activist — who was also his mistress's aunt.

Ever wonder how politics is downstream from social culture? Do you understand a little more as to why Black women make up a disproportionate number of abortions in the United States?

Let's move on to another big Liberal talking point:

Freedom of Expression

We have understood that in the past, freedom of expression meant that you could openly practice your religion and faith without worry or fear of persecution. What it refers to is that the individual is free to express their thoughts, beliefs, ideas, and emotions free from government censorship. There has been meaningful change that was instilled in our countries over the last eighty years, and the culmination of such was in the 50s and 60s through civil rights movements such as Rosa Parks, Martin Luther King Jr., Vietnam War protests, Women's Rights movement, and my favorite, Environmentalism.

While it looks great on paper, some of these movements were ill-conceived, and many who stood behind them had no idea for which they were fighting. Rosa Parks and Martin Luther King Jr. were incredible individuals who stood up to persecution and came out victorious, although not without the price being paid for the good Doctor. Women's rights protests were also just, in that both men and women should always be treated as equals. Unfortunately, what spawned from this movement was an irrational hatred for men by some of these women, who believed that it was their duty to succeed at all costs to prove that they belonged in the workforce as well. Sure, I have nothing against women in the workforce. In fact, I welcome it, and most women bring a certain aura of grace and friendliness with them. It caused men to learn to behave more appropriately in the workplace, namely, to stop acting like pigs. Even though some men still think of women as objects, the majority of workplaces are safe from major indecencies. The more powerful the men, the stupider they behave. Power corrupts after all. This movement later turned into what we know now as feminism. Unfortunately, that becomes a problem. See, in the days before women were able to work, all economics, finances, families, school systems, and workdays were designed to have one sole breadwinner in the household. The way that our society was designed in the 40s and 50s was based on the nuclear family dynamic with one wage earner in the home and for a very specific reason. It was seen as an important duty for wives to look after children and to keep their house a home. Feminists hate this because they believed it was a form of segregation to force women to raise children and to stay at home. Little did they realize that most women are very happy staying home looking after the family and taking care of their children and husbands. There is nothing more important in my opinion, than knowing there is one person in the family that keeps everyone together.

When children grow up with at least one parent in the home, statistically they are less likely to: drop out of school, commit crimes, or have children out of wedlock. When both parents are working, you put your faith and trust into the hands of certified strangers that have been recognized by someone at some point that they are qualified to raise your children for you, without having to deal with any of the consequences. This becomes increasingly more difficult when it is a one-parent household. Children, especially males, are five times more likely to commit crimes, drop out, or be promiscuous without any fear or repercussions. After all, who is to stop them? Do you think they know the love of their parents when the parents are never home? It may not sound fair since the single parent has to work to provide for the family, however, the child has no idea how to express how their lives have been impacted based on their parents' poor decision-making skills. This will trickle down to the child, creating a void of responsibility.

What ended up happening when women took to the workforce in large numbers in the '60s nearly put an end to the single-family breadwinner, because men and women were now competing for the jobs against each other. It was not like double the number of jobs suddenly became available. What happened was if a woman was hired in place of a man, oftentimes that meant that the man's family now had no source of income to keep their family afloat. This was the rise of the middle and upper middle class when both men and women in the family were working good-paying jobs, it created a large disposable income, and the family with no main earner was struggling.

Because of this, the wonderful government saw a need for increased social services. In comes welfare. Now those who don't work do not have to worry about how they will provide food and shelter for their family. The government will help lift that burden with social programs and increased taxes for those who are working. It was a solution to a problem that should have been worked out slowly, but typically when a new movement gets incredible momentum, they plow right through any rational thought like a tsunami washing away any opposing opinions. Now this welfare program really helped those who are single parents as well, allowing some of them to stay home and look after their children if an unfortunate circumstance happened in their lives like a spouse dying for example. However, this would soon start being taken advantage of by all of those who had children out of wedlock and now had one or more children to look after but no means to do it. That's OK, here comes the Big Brother government to help! Rather than encourage couples that had children because either they are unable to attain contraceptives or are stupid (sex without consequences) by creating social programs to assist in counseling for couples and unwed individuals who share a life, the great idea of child support came into play. Now instead of the child having both parents in their lives, the court will decide who has how much time to spend with them and force the father to pay support to the mother based on his income and their lifestyle. This system is not perfect of course… What happens when the father has no job? or is in jail? or disappears? not a damn thing. This has encouraged more single-parent families in the last 50 years more than any other reason. If you absolve people of responsibility, they will not act responsibly. WHO KNEW!

Now feminists have championed the movement from the 60s as a necessity to get women into the workforce, shaming those who choose to live the life of homemaker and caregiver. Is it sexist for my wife to cook me dinner and look after the children while I work? Only if you are an asshole who has never known happiness. My wife does these things, and she is well appreciated for it, while I constantly reassure her that we have made the right decision in choosing to raise our children ourselves and that

55

financially we will struggle for a little bit, but as they grow up it will ease. There are many women who dream of being able to do what my wife is able to do but always worry due to the economic climate, social status, careers, whether their spouse will make enough money to hold them afloat, and any other issues that may arise. Very few people plan that far ahead in their lives. Even in 2021, one of the biggest turn-ons for women is a man that makes enough money to sustain both his and his wife's lifestyles enough that if they bring a child into the world, it will not cripple them. So, if you hate the current situations of having to work and never seeing your children except for one hour in the morning and 2 hours in the evening, and not being able to afford property because of skyrocketing prices, thank a liberal. Instead of helping keep the family together, they prefer the social program way and abstain from responsibility.

The popular movements about Transgender rights, gender identity, spectrum... I don't even care anymore, and it's not because these social issues are less important than others, it is because there is no room for debate and logical thought to enter conversations. There is a drive to push a singular narrative down on everyone and it is a dangerous precedent. Rather than getting the care individuals require, they are being encouraged to cause self-harm in the form of mastectomies and genital mutilation all because they are encouraged to believe in something not rooted in factual evidence. If you really pay attention, you will realize that it has nothing to do with rights, but everything to do with being told how to think and feel about issues that you care little about. When these things become the topic of celebration and the traditional family goes out the window, the death of civilized society is not far away. During peace, the culture dramatically shifts, and during war, society is brought together. The last three generations have not known war to such an extent as in the 1940s.

Speaking of wars... the Vietnam War was a shit show. So many brave men died for a cause that many Americans did not understand. It started when the US government faked one of its vessels being attacked in the South China Sea and mobilized its army to go to war in Vietnam. I won't bore you with the details, but long story short: the US goes to war, and people in the US protest the war. The US withdrew from the war, civil unrest continued to the point that nearly two million more Vietnamese lost their lives. The entire reason the US entered that war was to assist Vietnam in holding its first-ever democratic elections, but the controlling interest in Vietnam refused to let that happen. This all escalated from the end of the Indochina war which was fought by French and Communist authorities at the time, lasting from 1949-1954. America's ultimate goal was to help secure democratic elections in the Country as much of it was divided from the Indochina war. The country was split between communist authorities that were backed by the Soviets and Chinese, and the Vietminh which was the Vietnamese Independence League. Ultimately, there was never a chance to strike peace between the warring bodies, and the US stepped in to quell the fighting, for the people back home, all they saw was that the US was sticking their nose into another country's business and that the US had no reason to interfere. By the end of it all, 56,555 US soldiers died, and 303,654 were wounded. Over 200,000 Saigon soldiers died, over 1 million North Vietnamese Soldiers dead, and half a million civilians. Approximately ten million became refugees. It's as if communism had a hold over the US citizens even during the Cold War, and people knew it.

From within the government, to its citizens, Socialism and

Communism were likened by many individuals, and it has created the most harm on the planet in the last one hundred years. But sure, let's keep trying folks! The Liberals will find a way!

To be quite honest, the reason why conservatives and religious people have been losing ground for decades is because the Liberals have a monopoly on people's emotions. Emotional responses to logical problems are what drive politics and culture. Not a shred of proof is needed to crucify someone, so long as they said something at some point that was taken out of context, and now you are out to ruin their lives. There will be a reaction of visceral hatred when I state that a man and a woman are needed in the family dynamic to raise children, even though it has been proven with statistics and research. There will be massive rage against all of those who do not take pronouns seriously. Quite frankly, if a person calls you something you don't identify as and it ruins your life, your life sucked long before you had that interaction. Want to know another unpopular but necessary and true opinion? Jesus saves.

All of the mental anguish and hatred going on in our society in the last twenty years can easily be solved with some time spent with the Lord. Another fun fact is that those who attend Christian Church regularly, have twenty times better mental health than those who do not know the Lord. Did I make that up? There was a Gallup poll done and asked individuals to personally rank their mental health. Majority of church goers rated their mental health as excellent or good compared to any other demographic. What seems like me pushing religion is just a mere statement that Jesus can help with any and all problems we face daily. Religion itself is a problem as well because so many lose themselves in worldly rules and ideologies and forget that God is not just rules and laws, but relationships. When you learn to have a healthy relationship with God, everything else will fall into place.

Religion teaches you that there is something you must do to be saved, how to pray, when to pray, and what you can and cannot eat. There are 613 rules in the Old Testament. Those who aim to keep and abide by all the laws written do it with such fervor that they lose sight of what God is all about. It was the religious Pharisees who killed Jesus because they would not accept him as God and called him a Blasphemer and only because the prophecies they studied for so many years were not fulfilled to the specifics they had envisioned. Even those who keep the rules and laws lose sight of what they are for. This is the entire purpose of Faith.

How you feel about right and wrong is irrelevant. The truth is the only thing that matters. God's word is law in the Old Testament (or Torah), but Jesus came to this world to help everyone understand the word of God and to bring about a massive change in the world through love. People to this day know the name Jesus all over the world more than any other person in history. Jesus is a name that will be criticized by those who scoff and loved by those who believe. Regardless of how you feel about Jesus, the Truth is absolute. If you find flaws in the bible there is one absolute truth you need to understand.

If you do not agree with God's word, you are the one in need of change. Reforming His word to better suit your vices will not help you. When a parent tells their child that they need to eat vegetables to be healthy, no matter how many times the child disagrees with them, the truth remains the same. No matter how much you choose to disagree with the Father's word, it will not make you right. Liberalism has decided that it is much more acceptable to permit all acts of debauchery than to follow God's word. Of course, who wants to be held down by stuffy rules that put family and self-preservation and worshiping God? Is it not better to be flamboyant in your sexual urges, your financial goals, and your love of self? Everything in the Liberal handbook is designed to contradict all of God's words, and for good reason.

In the name of progress and social acceptance, people have given way to the noisy few who wanted to be perverse in their pride rather than have humility and decency. Because of this, many with a secular worldview do whatever feels good to them without any regard for what they are doing to themselves. The 1960s were a tipping point for cultural acceptance and tolerance of the perverse. Many who were raised during these years paved the way for the destruction of civilization through three major events going through the world at this time. The sexual revolution, mainstream teaching of evolution, and the beginning of state-sponsored media. Allow me to briefly explain these three points.

The sexual revolution normalized debauchery. It brought about an abnormal amount of sexual experimentation through orgies and homosexual activity, lowered inhibitions, and incredibly high drug use. The young generation in the 60s believed that because we were placed on this earth for a short time, it was more important to try everything and have fun, regardless of the consequences. What brought about this thinking was the introduction of mainstream teachings of evolution. What better way to destroy people's values or morals, than to tell them they were not put on this planet by God, but were born and evolved from a bunch of happy accidents and coincidences that eventually led to the evolution of man from ape, meaning that we are nothing more than animals and it is perfectly justifiable to behave as such. This teaching brought about a new understanding that man-made rules, not God, Death brought man into the world not the other way around, and since the earth is billions of years old, we are improving every century instead of degrading every generation. How was it possible to convince an entire country that believed in God so much that it was written into the constitution and placed on its currency? Media and secular culture.

Almost all major media outlets in the world today started off as officers in the US military. Many of them received funding from the United States government to create infrastructure to control the airwaves and this crazy invention, the Television. It became much easier for any government entity to push propaganda through the media because no one thought that the government would ever lie to them for any reason and that everyone in the country was smart enough to form an educated opinion. Far from it actually. There are intelligent people, but a mass of ignorant people is a powerful tool to control. At the time of JFK's assassination, the CIA coined the term 'Conspiracy Theory', aiming to discredit anyone who had any type of opinion or evidence that would contradict the narrative being pushed by the media-run government. Many reporters aimed at getting to the truth, but today many reporters are just telling the same story in a creative new way. Hitler used newspapers and radio to convince his entire population that the cause of all strife in Germany was caused by Jews. Stalin used newspapers and radio along with strong military force to convince the Soviet Union that his dictatorship and forceful push for communism was to be done for the greater good of its citizens. North Korea today uses radio, TV, and mass broadcasting through loudspeakers to brainwash its citizens into believing that the Kim's are gods, and they need to be worshiped. Those who are caught with a bible are executed. Those caught with an American movie are executed. Those who

61

speak ill of the Kim's are executed.

Three major events that coincided together nearly sixty-years-ago set a course for the destruction of civilized society. Governments all over the world are aiming (and mostly succeeding) in passing 'Hate Speech' laws. In theory, which sounds great, but in practicality, this means that if you speak ill of the government, they will track you down and arrest you. This is now happening in Australia, France, Germany, England, Canada, Italy, and China to name a few. Besides China, which has been doing this for the last hundred years, Western countries have implemented strict speech rules to conveniently coincide with COVID-19 rules and regulations. Any dissident information that is not state-sponsored is flagged as fake news/hate speech/misinformation, and police are sent to your door to arrest you. What most do not realize is that the veil of lies given to the public is 'For your protection' or 'We are all in this together' or 'Flatten the curve'. This has been a successful test for the world powers to see how far they are able to push civilization to cooperate and to succumb to tyranny solely based on a false narrative. As COVID-19 has been a very real threat to the world, the solution was discovered mere weeks after a mass world spread, and just a few months after the worldwide lockdowns, an effective treatment was discovered in the form of Ivermectin and Hydroxychloroquine. Front-line doctors attempted to publish their findings but were silenced. Many doctors wanted to speak out and explain to the masses that there was a successful treatment discovered and significantly reduced symptoms and death but were not able to speak or send messages as Google, Twitter, and Facebook quickly flagged them and destroyed all records of their online existence.

For the first time in history, rather than listening to doctors and actual experts in the field of medicine, public sector figures who have not worked in the medical field for decades were suddenly creating all public policies regarding how to deal with the pandemic. Did no one find it odd that for the first time in history, all you were being told was that if you have the virus, stay in your house for two weeks and isolate? Your only options were to sit at home and let the virus run its course or go to the hospital and be placed on a ventilator if symptoms became severe. From that point, it was a race to see who could release a vaccine first. It seems like a true miracle that a vaccine has been created in a mere seven months from the onset of a global pandemic when just years prior it would take any pharmaceutical company years to develop and do trial runs. Not only that, but something that the world did not know about until January of 2020, now completely trust a mass-produced solution 11 months from first discovering the virus (allegedly)?

When did critical thinking fly out the window, I wonder...

Those who blindly believe everything they are told, sure have a funny way of calling those who are skeptical of such breakthroughs the conspiracy theorists. The lies people believe if repeated often enough are astounding. Goebbels was right. Even in Germany in the 1930s, the citizens were convinced that they were doing a public service by telling the Gestapo where the Jews lived and who they were. Those who do not know their history are doomed to repeat it. Personally, I think all of this requires tremendous faith to believe. It is truly shocking how this is easier to believe but struggle to believe in God. Often the Truth is very simple. Those who think it is too simple and need a complicated explanation are often wrong, however, they are seen as geniuses by their peers. If I believe in evolution and the people who evaluate my dissertation have the same fundamental beliefs, how is it possible that any critical thinking is allowed to happen in the first place? Ego and Pride are very complicated and many who suffer from them will never understand reality.

Try to understand that having faith in the wrong thing will surely lead to your demise. Therefore, it becomes incredibly important to discern those with good intentions and motives, and those with evil intentions and motives. It all comes down to Jesus. Once you understand that, everything becomes clear. I know it's not what most want to hear, but the truth is never easy to accept when it is avoided or rejected.

Wisdom and Humility vs. Knowledge and Pride

There is a very good reason why I write about all of these things, and there will be an explanation to all later on stemming from a mixture of experiences I have been through to form the opinions I currently hold.

The world is proud, and it is proud of the fact that it is proud. Pride is considered the greatest of all sins by God, and there is a good reason for it. Those who hold pride above all things harden their hearts, close their minds, and hurt those around them. To be humble is to know your place (literal meaning). As a parent, what do you try to teach the child who is too proud to apologize for causing pain to someone else? How does it make you feel when your peers cause you harm and do not apologize because they view that as a weakness? When your boss makes bad call after bad call causing you and your team to struggle needlessly and work overtime to fix his or her mistakes, what would make a world of difference to you that they are too proud to do?

Humility is one of the hardest things to have in one's character. It is a simple explanation, but a very difficult undertaking. How often do you feel that you are better than someone else because of your status in society or that some jobs are beneath you and you will never do because it is seen as embarrassing or contemptible? Wisdom and humility go hand in hand. You cannot become wise without first becoming humble. Wisdom is attained through the understanding that an individual always has much to learn about everything around them and is humble enough to accept that truth. When you get in a frame of mind that is open to learning from people you may disagree with on certain topics, you will come to understand that outside of your differences of opinion, there is something you are able to learn and retain simply by listening to their life experiences. When a child speaks to their parents, they have an understanding deep within them that knows that they are unable to process information on their own and need guidance from their parents in order to grow up with a better understanding of the world. When a person who has never been married seeks advice about marriage from a couple that has been together for thirty years, they are humble enough to accept that they do not know enough about marriage to successfully carry it out themselves, so they seek out those with the wisdom to teach them; and it turns to gain wisdom of their own. The single person who seeks counsel from their single friends or from their divorced parents is doomed to fail. Certain things in life you will not be able to learn from reading a book as words themselves are cold. However, once they are read aloud, the tone and depth of the words strike true for many.

On the other hand, those with knowledge may theoretically understand many concepts, but never have they put them into practice. It used to be that the only way to become a teacher in the past, was to have done significant work in the field of study to begin with. A Scholar did not become a scholar simply by reading books and interpreting them alone, they studied with the guidance of a mentor to show them the way, and after they ventured out on their own to apply that mixture of knowledge obtained from learning, and the wisdom attained from their mentor. Currently, in society, those who want to become teachers have no life experiences to bring forth. They finished high school, went to university, then off to teachers' college, and finally back to high school, but now to teach.

What can possibly be learned from those who have not gained any wisdom? Knowledge is attainable by all, but without wisdom, there can be no understanding of the knowledge learned. Those who lack wisdom lack humility. Those with knowledge and no humility become boastful and full of pride. Once your heart is filled with pride, you close off your mind to those who have a differing opinion, causing you to resent their point of view without even taking the time to listen. Incomplete opinions are formed, and ignorant statements are made due to a lack of wisdom. Now we see those celebrating their pride. They celebrate ignorance and sin while scoffing at those who have wisdom to share and humility to teach. If you aim to just celebrate those things in your life that make you feel good and have no understanding of them, you will never fill that emptiness in your soul that craves something more. No number of friends, money, or sexual deviancy will fill that void. If you want to know what it's truly like to be happy, volunteer at a retirement home and speak to some residents who are warm and inviting. You will come to understand what life is really all about, and you can save yourself YEARS of learning if you humble yourself and listen to the wise who lived through it. There will be those who are miserable, and you will be destined to follow them and end up like them if you do not heed the words of the wise.

There was a time in my life when I closed myself off to my mother, who was the only family I had left at the time. She came to Christ and wanted me to listen to her testimony. I was stubborn and ignorant as a young man, thinking that I knew better than her and that she was brainwashed into believing in Jesus. The thing about mothers is, they are patient and loving even if you reject them. She prayed for me a lot. I thought she was losing her mind. It took a while but finally, I came around and gave it a chance. Even though at the time I believed that I had more knowledge than my mother, I was not humble enough to listen to the wisdom she attained. It was a good thing she was patient. Wise people tend to have much more patience than those who think they know everything and are too proud to admit otherwise.

Education, Experience, and Motivation

These two things cannot exist without each other, and yet separately they are useless. Think of an amateur golfer for instance. Many are those who understand the theory of golf technique; how to play by the rules of the game, how to swing, how to putt, which club to use, and how much force to use… it makes no difference if you cannot apply that education without getting in the practice. Practice is experience. There is an old saying; that to become proficient in something, you need to spend 10,000 hours doing it. You can learn how to read music, but what good does that do you when you have never touched an instrument? What use is knowing how to build a fence or a deck if you have never held a hammer or drill? Education is extremely important, but education without experience is not true education. One cannot exist to its full potential without the other, especially if you are not motivated enough to continue.

Ask a golfer how many hours they would spend at the driving range forcing their body to do what they need in order to get that perfect swing. Ask a chef how many hours of chopping vegetables they have done in order to be as quick and proficient at the task. Talk to a farmer and ask what good theory does for them if the weather is not perfect. Gaining experience helps us adapt to a situation that education cannot give us.

On the flip side, without learning those golf techniques, you can swing for 10,000 hours and still have terrible form. You might get lucky and be able to hit the ball, but you have no concept of how to improve without a teacher who has both experience and education. The same goes for the chef who knows how to chop 50 lbs. of onions in ten minutes but has no idea how to apply heat, time, or technique to his cooking skill in order to make something out of raw ingredients. There are many upon many cooks who can grill a fantastic steak on the grill they have worked on for years but give them a different set of equipment and it will be like watching a fish out of water. They do not have the education to understand how to apply techniques to other types of equipment to get similar results. The farmer needs a solid blend of experience and education in order to succeed. Growing crops is not as easy as most would think. There are a lot of variables that go into growing food, and the hardest variables are the ones you cannot control but must adapt to.

This fits in perfectly with humility and wisdom to gain the experience you need in order to succeed at anything you attempt. Learn from a pro, learn from a book, practice, and ask questions. It can become very frustrating to see so much effort put into a task that is not turning out the way you planned. Giving up is easy. Staying motivated enough to practice until it works for you is hard. Every job on this planet has a learning curve. Find the master to help guide you, as their wisdom will enlighten you in a way you may never have thought of on your own.

How to Apply it All

The reason I spent so long explaining many things before getting into details on how to live the life you want without stress or anxiety, is because you need to have a certain approach when it comes to understanding my way of thinking. I am not a genius by any stretch of the imagination. I consider myself an average guy with an average dream and average goals. I want to live my life comfortably enough that I don't have to worry about finances, happy that I can balance my life around work and family, and slowly build some material and spiritual wealth in the process.

Forget what you think you know about the workforce.

Forget about being rich or famous.

Forget about having expensive luxuries or status.

Clear your mind of such frivolities and focus on what you know to be capable of.

As an adult, I will assume that you fall into 1 of 3 types of people when it comes to life. Reckless, Responsible, or Clueless.

A Reckless individual will charge headfirst into any situation that they deem to have even a slight interest in. They do not manage money well, they have a short attention span, and they focus all their attention on the goal of making money. They can survive on their own, but life will always be difficult since there is no guidance on how to curb impulsive behavior. A clueless person will explode and get frustrated often, as a reckless person has a difficult time explaining rationality to someone who has no idea what is going on. Reckless and Responsible people together can thrive as the responsible person helps tame that impulse and bring some reason and patience into the relationship. Two reckless people together are just going to compound the problem. This relationship is what you see when both people always want the best no matter the cost, often getting into massive debt because of their lust for material gain.

The Clueless person simply has no idea what to do with their life and always needs guidance or direction. They can survive and thrive with a responsible person guiding them and directing them, but they cannot survive on their own. This type of person has no concept of how to formulate a budget, no idea how to live within their means, and is the easiest to take advantage of. They will feel incompetent with a reckless person as they will feel they cannot keep up and don't know how to express their desires or frustrations. Two Clueless people together is painful to watch. Bad decisions on top of bad decisions get made, and debt follows because one cannot guide the other. They both learn from trial and error, but unfortunately not after the first error. They will fail multiple times at the same thing until they have a small semblance of realization.

Responsible people are pretty self-explanatory. These types of people have a good grasp on how to budget their finances, and the work they need to put into anything to be successful at it, and they can formulate plans well into the future to be able to make smart, calculated, and safe decisions. Two responsible people together will have a fantastic grasp of their finances, they will plan together on how to spend money, and they will assess risk before taking any unnecessary steps in their lives. Some might think of this as boring, and it very well may be for most. However, since both of them will have similar goals due to their responsible nature, Life will be easier.

So now how do we become responsible in life? What are all the things you need to know about how to live your life in the Western world at this point in time?

I will attempt to break it down from the point of your last years in high school. Ideally, this is the best starting point before you have had the chance to make some truly terrible decisions, but I will also work on how to course correct if you are finding yourself stuck in a hole you can't get out of. The first thing I will ask is that you put down the shovel. You can't dig your way out of a hole, you have to slowly climb out.

You may have realized which category of person you belong to. It's better that you do because if you think everything is fine and you are swamped with debt, you have been paying rent for the last ten years, or you have nothing to your name, it's time to reassess your life. The reason I talked about my life was to give you an understanding of how I came to these conclusions and why I found it necessary to teach some that are lost. I am not perfect, but reflecting on my life so far, I believe that I can help guide those who struggle just to have an average dream. I will bring each topic down to the level at which I understand it and can help you understand it through personal experience and reflection.

The Importance of Studying and Hard Work

"Reading maketh a full man; conference a ready man; and writing an exact man." - Sir Francis Bacon

Studying and hard work are two important factors that contribute to success in both personal and professional aspects of life. While some people may possess innate talents and abilities, those who are willing to put in the time and effort to learn and grow will likely be more successful in the long run. The most important factor to take into account is that studying is a critical component of personal and professional growth. Whether one is pursuing academic or professional goals, it is essential to gain knowledge and skills in a specific field or discipline. Studying allows individuals to acquire knowledge, develop critical thinking skills, and expand their understanding of the world around them. By dedicating time and energy to studying, individuals can deepen their understanding of a subject, become better problem solvers, and improve their ability to communicate effectively with others. Hard work is necessary to achieve success in any field. Success rarely comes easy, and individuals who are willing to put in the effort and perseverance to achieve their goals are more likely to succeed than those who do not. Hard work is necessary to achieve mastery in any field, and it takes dedication, discipline, and persistence to achieve success. Whether one is pursuing a career, starting a business, or pursuing personal goals, hard work is an essential ingredient for success. These are also important for building self-confidence and self-esteem. When individuals work hard and achieve success, they gain a sense of accomplishment and pride in their work. This feeling of achievement can boost their self-confidence and help them overcome challenges and obstacles they may encounter in the future. Additionally, these traits can help individuals build a strong work ethic, which is essential for success in any field. They are important for developing critical thinking skills. When individuals study and work hard, they are forced to think critically about problems and come up with creative solutions. This type of thinking is essential for success in any field, as it allows individuals to tackle complex issues and develop innovative ideas that can lead to success.

Critical thinking skills are necessary for making informed decisions, and individuals who possess these skills are better equipped to make sound judgments and choices. Another reason why studying and hard work are essential for success is that they help individuals develop resilience. Life is full of challenges and setbacks, and individuals who are willing to work hard and persevere through difficult times are more likely to overcome these obstacles and achieve success. Resilience is an essential trait for success, as it allows individuals to bounce back from failure and setbacks and continue moving forward towards their goals. This way of thinking and habit-building is important for developing a growth mindset. A growth mindset is the belief that one's abilities and intelligence can be developed through hard work and dedication. Individuals with a growth mindset are more likely to view challenges and obstacles as opportunities for growth and improvement, rather than as roadblocks to success. This type of mindset is essential for success, as it allows individuals to embrace new challenges and take risks that can lead to success. When individuals pursue their goals with dedication and hard work, they are more likely to achieve a sense of satisfaction and fulfillment in their lives. This sense of purpose can motivate individuals to continue working hard and striving towards their goals, even in the face of challenges and setbacks.

Understanding your Limitations

"I know that I am intelligent, because I know that I know nothing." – Socrates

"The fool doth think he is wise, but the wise man knows himself to be a fool." – William Shakespeare

Don't misunderstand, the idea behind this is that we can see for ourselves even in high school those who will succeed, those who will just get by, and those who will struggle… and there will be a lot of struggling. it is vital that you find an interest of yours that you can actually perform well and can make money doing it. Prostitution or gambling is not a skill, FYI. Ultimate Frisbee or Gender Studies, for example, will not help you in your life either.

Many kids fail to realize how important it is to find a type of career that they have an interest in that will not consume their lives. The goal is to find a type of job that you can see yourself doing because you can excel at it, but not something that you love so much you will be disheartened if it does not turn out exactly as you had in mind. If you love to learn about medicine but have shaky hands, good to realize now that being a surgeon is not a good idea. However, in the field of medicine with your limitations, there are many other jobs that can be enjoyable. Do not limit your thinking to just one profession within one field of study. Doctors are not all working in hospitals. Family practice, pediatrics, specialties, pharmaceuticals, or even consultants have their place.

If you want to be a chef, for example, understand that there is a world outside of restaurants and hotels. You can do catering, retirement, mass production, cruise ships, airlines, large third-party suppliers or manufacturers of kitchen equipment, consultants, instructors, or private Chefs to name a few. If you limit yourself to one option, you limit your chances of gaining the experience and education you need to achieve a well-rounded career.

So, what do you do if you have no current aspirations or career goals?

Look at websites that give detailed information as to what professions are currently in high demand, and which professions are growing in popularity. What you will notice is that these two lists are not the same, meaning that what is currently popular is not useful. Do some detailed research on the most in-demand jobs to find out which appeals to you the most and pursue it. You can make countless excuses for yourself that you do not think this is the right choice for you, or that it doesn't make as much money as you hoped it would, but that way of thinking is irrelevant. You will never get the money you expect when you start green in a new career, and you will never fall in love with your career path immediately. When you Pick a career that you have any interest in, this will make it much easier to continue doing it and that motivation will help you improve as time goes on. In 2022, the most in-demand jobs at this moment are:

Construction Estimator
Financial Advisor
Home Health Aide
Electrician
Medical Technologist

Nursing Assistant
Occupational Therapist
Pharmacist
Physical Therapy Aide
Pipefitter
Registered Nurse
Software Engineer
Statistician
Truck Driver
Web Developer

Personally, I have no interest in any of these jobs, but if I were to pick one, it would be a truck driver. There is minimal schooling involved with basic requirements, and it pays very well from the start. The downside for me is driving long haul since I like to be home every night, but there are many jobs offered that do not require such commitments.

When you do your research, commit to your favorite from the list you find, and you will succeed. When you have stable work, or you want to pursue something else, you will always have a good fallback plan if your new choice does not work out.

You will always hear such nonsensical phrases like: "Chase your Dreams!" or "If you can dream it, you can do it." Or even "You can do anything you set your mind to."

While it may sound very motivational, it is also deceptive. It does not set realistic goals for you because there are two people who know you better than you know yourself, and those are your parents. (I will not be getting into broken home families or absent parents. Apply this information to your life as closely as it relates to it). Have a positive discussion with them and ask what they think you are good at and what they think you struggle with. The first step to attaining wisdom is to understand that negative feedback is not meant to bring you down but to help you overcome problems by addressing them. Some parents will not be good with this and may make jokes or try to make fun of you for it but remember that this does not reflect on your shortcomings but on theirs. If they find pleasure in telling you what you are bad at, then it would be a better idea to ask for that information from someone you trust to give you an honest answer.

On a side note, whether you had a bad or good childhood, you know what you like and dislike about how your parents raised you. Do better when your time comes.

If you know that the feedback you receive has truth to it, do not shy away from it but let it help you determine what the right path for you to follow is. Are you a bad driver, avoid transport trucks... are your math skills leaving something to be desired? It might be a wise idea to move past your desire to become a Financial Advisor. Pick something in your wheelhouse that you know you can succeed in.

Seeking Wise Counsel

One interesting piece of advice I came across was from listening to Pastor Mark's podcast, specifically, his Spirit-Filled Jesus sermons. He spoke about meeting a gentleman who has never had a formal education, went through financial pain, and relational pain, and started with nothing. Over time, this man had become a highly successful business leader, very wise, very godly, and very generous. How did it all happen? The man said to Mark that the greatest thing he has done in his life to help him turn his life around was to seek people with wisdom.

Seek People with Wisdom

How important this is cannot be stressed enough. Knowledge is meaningless without wisdom. How is it possible to get from nothing to everything? You cannot judge someone based on where they are at but understand better the progress they have made. This man sought wise counsel. He met with people who knew what to offer and he attentively listened, took notes, and applied them to his life. He gave Mark a very practical answer (In summary). "My plan has always been the same. When I meet someone who has wisdom in an area of life, I pray about meeting with them. And if I feel like the Lord would want that, I ask them 'Can I meet with you.' I then scheduled a meeting. I show up early because I want to honor their time. At the beginning of the meeting, I ask them how much time they have, because I want to respect that, and I always carry a notebook with me. I feel like the world is a classroom and school is always in session, and if I see something or if I learn something I write it down. I have categories for Family, Finances, Health, for the Lord, and I make notes and collect all of that, and I journal it out because I am always looking to learn. Any questions I have before the meeting I write them down, I will ask them the questions, and I let them do most of the talking. When they say something I write it down, and If I think it is a good action item, I make a commitment to them that I will go and do it. I ask them at the end of the meeting if there is anything else they want to share, and I pray for them and I thank them, and I ask them if I do these things and I have more questions, would you be willing to meet with me again? I have been doing this for decades. Everything I know, this is how I learned it." It is incredibly simple, and yet very difficult for most to wrap their heads around the effort you need to put into your life. Mark goes on to ask how it works for him if someone approaches him with questions or requests his time. "If somebody shows up late, that is a problem. If they wait until it is a crisis and run into my life rather than respecting my time, that's a problem. If I meet with them, and they are on their phone, that is a problem. If they do not write anything down, that's a problem. If I give them an assignment and they do not do it, that's a problem." Mark asked if he meets with those types of people, and the man responded, "Not Twice." That is wisdom.

You must understand that opportunity is not a right, it is a privilege. No one on this planet is responsible for you besides yourself as an adult. If you do not show interest or respect for those who teach you, they will distance themselves from you. Approach every situation with wise counsel, humility and respect. You will earn a lot. I recommend checking out the Real Faith app or picking up a copy of Spirit-Filled Jesus by Mark Driscoll if you want a deeper dive. It has done a lot for me; I am sure it will help you in some way.

The Trades

"Choose a job you love, and you will never have to work a day in your life." – Confucius

"Skilled workers are not cheap. Cheap workers are not skilled." – Unknown

"Work is the grand cure of all the maladies and miseries that ever beset mankind." – Thomas Carlyle

Turn your interest into your passion. There are a wide variety of useful trades that have been created and mastered over the last thousand years. Obviously, some like blacksmiths, goldsmiths, or tanners are not exactly in demand, but they could be excellent hobbies to pursue down the road. Picking a hobby is not the goal. Picking a job that you enjoy and could see yourself putting countless hours into is the goal.

Every trade that is available to learn from your local college will always be useful, regardless of the fears that certain individuals place on the general population regarding their future existence. As wonderful as it sounds to have a world of robots that take all the skilled jobs of the many, that is not exactly a reality, not even for the next 50 years at least. While it is true that robotics and automation have improved consistency in material goods, that is not something that drives motivation for a growing economy, only because it still requires the creativity and skill to program all of the robotics to perform the tasks delegated. Think of it this way: What are some things that exist now and will continue to be in demand regardless of growing tech? Do you think that any tech would exist if it was not piggybacked off a service that was necessary?

Houses will always be in need. To build, to repair, to restore. What Jobs are required for regular home maintenance? HVACs, electricians, and Plumbers are quite possibly the most valued as the majority of problems we will encounter in our lifetimes require at least one of these professions to be involved. Installing A/C, furnace, or having issues with them? HVAC. Need to add a Breaker to increase the power for a specific appliance? Electrician. Any issues related to water? Plumber. (This one will be the most in need because Water damage can have severe repercussions).

Cars will always need maintenance (Whether it is internal combustion or electric or possibly hydrogen fuel cells)

Clothes will always need to be purchased and worn. Like fashion? Great. Learn how to mend, repair, and create.

Think about recreational activities the masses enjoy and what it takes to keep them operational. Amusement parks (What do they all have? Amusements! Animatronics, Rides, Waterparks, interactive displays etc.)

Think about commodities that are always in demand and disposable. Not disposable right away, but you know for a fact that many people will be buying more than one in their lifetime. (Such as shoes, pens, pencils, tablets, storage containers, paint, food, toiletries, cleaning supplies etc.... so many options to specialize in that will never leave you without work).

Perhaps there is general building maintenance that needs to be performed on a large scale and requires electricians, HVAC, Carpenters, plumbers, pipefitters.

All the public service jobs (unfortunately union run but nothing is perfect...) that need to be filled.

What are all the types of things and services we all need? That is the focus of a career path that needs to be addressed. There is no point in giving detailed information on every profession. Do your research and find out what best suits your wants and needs. Just remember, at 18 you will not be thinking about family life, so that is the time to get your hands dirty and grind. When the time comes and you want to start a family, assess your choices and how they will impact what you will want at the period of your life.

Investing – In Yourself

"The day you plant the seed is not the day you eat the fruit." – Unknown

"An investment in knowledge pays the best interest." – Benjamin Franklin

I am a student, and the world is my classroom. Remember the story not too long ago about Mark Driscoll and his friend meeting up to talk? This is the perfect time to read carefully.

Oddly enough, investing does not just mean using your money to make a profit down the road, it also means taking the time to invest in yourself with knowledge and experiences. If you have been 'encouraged' into going to college or university, truly assess your goals before you spend that amount of money on a degree or diploma that may be of no use to you when you attain it. As I said before, there are jobs that will never go away, and there will always be a need for skilled workers. If you invest your time to learn a trade, that will never go to waste. On the other hand, life experiences do not spontaneously arrive at your feet, you must go out and force that experience upon yourself. How will you ever go explore Europe or Asia if you sit at home and contemplate existence? Get off your ass, work and save money to do a comfortable trip for several months and really take in something that only a few dares try anymore.

Personally, I was able to use my education and experience to work for a cruise company and explore the world while working for them. Best decision of my life. Not only did I get to experience a multitude of diverse cultures and ways of life, but I did it all while getting paid. There were many times that I became incredibly frustrated with the working conditions and management because they would treat the crew like shit, but if I was not fighting with them, I was exploring and learning every day. I met my wife during my time on the ships, and now we have three beautiful kids together.

If you do not have an aptitude for a trade, think of a creative way to share your interests with others or encourage those to take a leap of faith into the unknown to push forward and utilize that self-investment strategy. Look at how many multimedia opportunities there exist online. You can apply your interest in a creative way to display it to the world and make ample amounts of money while you do it. Trade not for you? learn how to market yourself. Learn how to edit videos, compose a playlist, share your art, or write what is on your mind.

It may be very difficult for some to hone in on what they want to do with their lives. If you are reading this and fall into that category, allow me to be your guidance counselor for a few minutes. Two things to start off with: Do you view yourself as a positive person or a negative person? If it is a negative person, let's address that first.

Your approach to life will be exactly what you get out of it. Glass half full/empty will always come to mind. There is nothing wrong with you being a negative person, it is that you have been conditioned to accept negativity, and in turn, it radiates from you. To be a positive person takes a lot of effort. If you do not want to change, then there is absolutely no reason why you should continue to read this book. If you have an ounce of interest in getting out of your slump and fortifying your mind to condition yourself to be joyful and positive, you need to understand that the road will not be an easy one, but it will be well worth the effort.

Let us begin by reconditioning your way of thinking. Write down the five things in your life you find that brings you the most joy. By things I do not just mean material items; it can be music, art, a special person, a place you go to, food you eat, the atmosphere you enjoy, reading this book... you name it! Once you identify five, reflect on how each thing makes you feel and what it does for you. Hold on to that feeling. Now, write down the five things that cause you grief and sadness.

Once you identify them, do your best to distance yourself from them as much as possible. Some instances may be very difficult to avoid if one of the reasons is your life at home, and that would require some help from a professional (not just phycologist, but perhaps a social worker or police... hopefully it is not that bad of a situation, but it if is please know that there are several ways you can get help, you just need to reach out to someone you trust and get it across to them how dire the situation is).

If the negative items are unavoidable, try to incorporate some of the things that bring you joy during the times you feel anxious or sad to help mitigate the difficulty and ease any suffering you experience. It is not easy to change your mindset to be positive, I completely understand. It requires a lot of effort, and it can be exceedingly difficult when you have no encouragement or support. Just know that you are not alone. Church is a fantastic place to help shake negativity, you just have to keep an open mind.

Once you identify the good and the bad and how it affects your mood, draw up a plan for yourself on how you can do those things that you love more often. What would it take for you to pursue something you have a deep affection for? If it is a specific job, work on learning the key skills needed to achieve it. If you have the skills but not the attitude, look for a mindset coach and involve yourself in more positive groups that help lift you up. Staying away from Reddit chatrooms or Facebook comments will help with this. Being around positive people will help with this. Remember, one of the keys to changing your perception of yourself, is to be around the types of people you want to be like. If you associate with drug addicts or criminals, the likelihood you will become one is remarkably high. If you surround yourself with encouragement, praise, confidence, and love, what are the chances you will start to emulate those feelings towards others? This is referred to as 'success or failure by association.'

The rise or fall of your dreams is dependent on the association you build around yourself. You want to have the opportunity to create an environment around yourself that will help encourage and nurture positivity. I know I sound repetitive and perhaps pushy but find a good Church. There are so many wonderful people you will find and encourage you to connect on a deeper level, you will be surprised what kind of friendships you form and how that will positively affect your life.

Once you have attained a positive mindset, look at your list again. Do a self-assessment on how those things affect you now. Are the negative aspects you had written down still crippling or manageable? You will see that problems can be solved in a multitude of ways, and it all depends on the lens you have on. Also, your problems will not seem like problems anymore but merely challenges you want to overcome and learn from.

Now think about what you want to do with your life. What do you want to contribute and what do you want to achieve? Making a list is a good start, but understand that the more you add to it, the more overwhelming it might seem, and it can also be crippling to see a large list, not know where to start, and just give up before even attempting one thing off it.

The better suggestion is to think of something important you want to achieve and make a list of the steps needed to get there. For example, I want to be able to take my entire family to Europe for a few weeks to soak in some culture and to visit distant relatives, however, I do not have the income to support that. The first thing I would do is set a goal or when I would like to travel. From there, I would work out what the current costs of things like hotel stays, plane tickets, food etc. are, and add 15 percent to that for a comfortable cushion of expenses. Once I have my number, I will decide how to attain a specific amount each year to add to the total I need. From that yearly savings, I would map out how much I need to set aside each month to make sure it is feasible.

Let us say that I want to save $10,000 in 4 years. That is $2500 per year, and in turn $208 per month. Unbelievably, that is an average of about $6.95 per day to set aside. Now, take that daily sum and deposit it into a small investment fund for yourself (many options out there, but a low-risk mutual fund would be the wisest choice if you don't want to dabble in the stock markets). let us say that your average return will be 6 percent a year (can be lower, but on average you will earn 6-12 percent depending on which you choose). so now you deposited 2500 in your first year and made 6 percent on that. I now have 2650. Add another 2500 to that investment with 6 percent interest on the entire amount. I now have 5459 saved. Another year goes by and another 2500 deposited. Six per cent of the total brings me to 8436. another year, another 2500 to the total plus 6 percent.

I now have 11,592 and change on the goal I made of saving 10,000. Oh look, I invested and gave myself a 15 percent cushion unintentionally.

Think how much money you spend on fast food, specialty drinks, video games, entertainment... Saving $7 a day can net you over 10,000 in 4 years. Do you think saving for a down payment on a mortgage is hard? What if you can set aside $15 a day? Today, that is 1 hour of work at a minimum-wage job in Canada. From an eight-hour day, are you strained to set aside earnings from 1 of those hours? Truly contemplate this for yourself and understand that this is only hard because you do not have the mindset to pursue the goal. Once you get in the right frame of mind, it is all possible. Remember, life is not a sprint to the finish. It is a journey that we need to experience, so take it slow, enjoy it, and plan for it for the best outcome for your best self.

The Road to Greatness starts with positivity

"Keep away from people who try to belittle your ambitions. Small people always do that, but the really great make you feel that you, too, can become great." – Mark Twain

"The final proof of greatness lies in being able to endure criticism without resentment." – Elbert Hubbard

"The purpose of life is not to be happy. It is to be useful, to be honorable, to be compassionate, to have it make some difference that you have lived and lived well." – Ralph Waldo Emerson

One day at a time. One word at a time. One thought at a time. Challenge yourself to be positive. It is amazingly simple to pick out something you do not like about a person, be it their hair, their shoes, their clothes, their make-up, their car, their music taste, their cooking, their lifestyle... It is also quite easy to pick out something nice to say to a person like complimenting their hair, their shoes, their clothes, their make-up, their music taste... you get the point.

Be genuine in your positivity. You don't have to like everything but make it a goal of yours to find SOMETHING positive and focus on that. You cannot stand a colleague of yours because they are two-faced? Compliment them. It may feel gut-wrenching at the time, but you will slowly see their attitude change if you strive to do it daily. Make it a genuine compliment, make it different every day, and make it brief. Positivity is contagious and more so than negativity because everybody wants to be around a positive person. And if they do not, that is an issue they need to solve personally. DO NOT let them affect you for the worse.

There was a time in my life when I would just stew over negativity. Any bad comment, any negative evaluation, or any unfavorable experience would live rent-free in my brain. There was no reason for it, but I was already programmed to accept negativity as my main source of mental nourishment. I would dread evaluations at work. Even though I knew I was lacking in certain areas, I would make excuses for myself that it was not me, it was the manager. It was their fault that I was not able to perform at a higher level due to poor coaching, poor training, or no communication. I would have the habit of doing the bare minimum and skating because I figured that if I was not performing at a reasonable level, they would tell me. The issue with this mentality is that when they would tell me, I would fight them on it or make excuses to the point that I would not change, I would just start resenting the manager giving me bad reviews. The most awkward thing to change about this habit is taking ownership of everything that you affect.

Did you show up late to work because of traffic? Leave earlier. There is traffic every day. Work that into your schedule.

Are you having a hard time focusing on work? Put the phone in airplane mode. Everyone you love and care about knows how to reach you at work if they really need you. Texting, checking Facebook, and watching TikTok lunacy is not conducive to helping you focus.

Not having a good relationship with fellow managers or co-workers? Share your opinions a little less. If there is a hot topic being discussed and you have opposing views on it and you are the minority, think to yourself what shouting it at them will accomplish. This is not the battleground for your opinions, so walk away.

Not a 'Team Player'? You will be surprised what the phrase "Can I give you a hand with anything" can do. Most of the time your help will be refused. Seldom is it needed. When it is, it will be appreciated that you asked and helped. As a manager, it is as simple as seeing your team scramble and just inserting yourself in a basic role that helps give them time for something else to focus on.

Are your assignments late? Ask your manager what items are the most pressing to complete and focus on them first. Answering emails can be done first thing in the morning, and last thing before you leave. No one needs a response within five minutes.

Is multitasking proving difficult? That is because it is not a real thing… As a human, you are not able to do multiple tasks at one time. Even if you think you are multitasking, you are still prioritizing one over another, or doing a half-assed job on multiple tasks. If you do not believe me, try watching two shows. Write down the dialogue in one of them. Now write down what happened in the one you were not paying attention to. Does it seem silly and impossible? That is because it is. You cannot go left and right at the same time. Pick a direction.

What most people interpret as multitasking is being able to listen, take notes, and input data at a quick pace.

Let us dive into multitasking a little. Take driving a manual car as an example (because automatics are jokes). You have the clutch, gear shift, brakes, and accelerator. Your feet, hands, and eyes all must work in tandem to be able to move the vehicle successfully. Even though there are many different motions and focuses all at once, the task remains simple: Driving. Let's not forget when it's nighttime to turn on the lights, wipers when it's raining, music to listen to, that coffee in your hand, that phone call you might take (Bluetooth of course), or even the noisy family members in your vehicle. If anything would be considered multitasking, Driving would be at the top of the list. So, calling clients, then calling contractors, conveying all necessary information, logging it, communicating any important information, and making sure all parties involved are satisfied with the results should not be a difficult feat to achieve. Take it one task at a time. You will ensure it is done correctly, efficiently, and most importantly... ONCE! You will learn that if you have time to scramble and do the task again, you have enough time to do it properly the first time.

Focus on What Matters

"Take therefore no thought for the morrow: for the morrow shall take thought for the things of itself. Sufficient unto the day is the evil thereof." – Matthew 6:34

"If I had an hour to solve a problem, I would spend 55 minutes thinking about the problem, and 5 minutes thinking about the solution" – Albert Einstein

I thought writing this book would be very straightforward. The number of things that get in the way is shocking. Even for me, focusing on completing the task gets overshadowed by a new, more pressing task in need of completion. The fact that you are reading this shows that it was finally accomplished so I can pat myself on the back for that, however, it was not without many, many distractions.

Within the months that I was on parental leave, I had a laundry list of things I wanted to accomplish before returning to work. I wanted to write this book (it got done since you are reading it so that's a good thing) learning to trade, learning to invest, learning affiliate marketing, learning how to lead a church group, supporting my mom and stepfather with their trials, supporting my wife through her doubts and fears, supporting my children, working on my own short-comings like lack of patience and clarity, cooking three meals a day for the family, planning family outings to get them out of the house, shopping for groceries and other necessities, and on, and on, and on…

When it comes to my family, should I focus on them or draft a book instead? Even though the answer is clear, I hesitate to make the right decision between something I want to do and something I must do. When trials come into your life that need resolution, focus on them. I do not mean focus on them and worry about it, I mean look for solutions, however small, and move forward in aiming to accomplish the task. It feels like a failure when you start a task and you do not see results quickly. It discourages many people from pursuing the task further. Whether it is that chosen career, that entrepreneurial venture, the self-help (more on that later), or just not understanding what you are being taught. When you are told that something you do should yield results in a specific timeframe and you do not achieve it, you will highly likely consider yourself a failure. Understand that everyone grasps information at various levels. I am particularly good at reading a social situation. I struggle with analytics and accounting. I am exceptionally good at teaching material I grasp very well and that will not be the case for all. There are certain individuals who are true geniuses and want to help others by getting that information out of their brains and teaching it. The trouble is, they make lousy teachers. A Genius goes from point A to F in their explanations and just does not understand why they need to explain B C D E along the way. What an educator should be able to do is learn from that genius and apply the knowledge in such a way that it can be understood by those they are trying to help. If you ever considered anyone in your life a genius but could not understand them for the life of you, this is why. If you ever watched The Big Bang Theory, the dynamic of Sheldon, Penny, and Leonard is a perfect example. The genius cannot teach or explain why he does what he does that makes sense to anyone but him. The educator interprets the genius and can understand and relay that information to others.

There is a reason some of the best sports players make terrible coaches. They cannot explain how to be great; they just are. Geniuses cannot explain why they are any more than you can explain to yourself why you like a certain food over another.

When you understand yourself and your learning capabilities, focusing on the tasks that are in front of you will be a lot less daunting and you will find success through your struggle. You may not be a genius with natural talents, but you can easily be a genius of hard work and use that focus to determine the outcome for which you are searching.

Focus requires determination. You will not be able to commit to something you do not have an interest in. To get a grasp on what you seek, clearly outline what it is that you are trying to achieve and map out a strategy in smaller parts to clearly see what is needed at every interval. Without a guide, you will lose focus because it will not be drawn to a specific point, it will be like a flag in the wind just flailing about wherever the wind blows.

Wants and needs to be revisited

When I observe my children and speak to them, it becomes noticeably clear that they do not need any guidance to be selfish. It is inherent. Whoever says that children are born pure, and we just need to guide their growth is an idiot, simply put. Those who have raised children know that although they are blessings, they are selfish, oblivious, destructive, and messy. Parents know all too well that children do not need any practice or coaching to quickly tell you many hundred times a day what they want. It is a parent's job to provide the child with what it needs first, not what it wants. How do we differentiate? With a lot of practice and self-control. This requires a lot of re-wiring in our brains to understand that the world is just a giant advertisement drawing your attention to spend your money on things you do not need. So, let's focus on needs first.

As the children of God, we are born with the blueprint to be great. We will not achieve greatness alone, that is why we have parents. Those without guidance struggle.

Physically, we need food and water, shelter, and clothing. That is basic and very simple. Our bodies need food and water for nutrition and fuel, primarily to have energy, grow, and maintain a healthy lifestyle. We all need a place to live. Whether it's a big house, a small apartment, or our parent's basement. Lastly, clothing is necessary because of human decency. There are very few instances where it is acceptable to walk around naked outside, and most of those instances are away from strangers. Let us face it, we only need three things to survive, so why do we crave more? In simple terms, it is because we are conditioned to covet things we do not need. If you need a car (most of us do) do you purchase something that will take care of your needs of transportation, or do you spend significantly more for a vehicle that is flashier with options you will never use?

When you look to buy a home, do you search for what you simply need for your family, or do you search for a better neighborhood, larger yard, two car garage, three or four bathrooms? Here is the truth: you never need more than two bathrooms. It is highly unlikely more than two people in your household need to poop at the same time for the same amount of time. If you take showers at the same time, you will quickly realize that your home does not have enough water pressure to be able to run both showers at full capacity. Most people will realize that even with the laundry machine running or the dishwasher their showers will not be as pleasant. One thing to remember is that with more income, you will be able to enjoy more luxuries than you want. Your mortgage should not be more than 30 percent of your income AFTER taxes. Sadly, banks will approve people for 39 percent before taxes. This will cripple you if that is what you decide. Let's break down all of the average costs per month that go into living in a house with three bedrooms, two bathrooms, and a family of four with an average of $5000 of income after taxes (This is a greater amount than most people have at their disposal, so it will give you a very good idea of where your money goes). You will understand how monthly payments stack up when you do not own any of the products below. This is the average debt structure most people find themselves in due to their wants above needs. Additional expenses do not necessarily mean you will spend money on all of them, just giving a sample of what it costs and where income will go.

As you will soon realize, the less you own, the more you pay monthly. This will destroy the average family and put them into debt, which then later they will need to leverage assets to pay it off. The structure that our society is set up with makes this the standard of living, and it keeps the middle class and the poor from ever attaining wealth solely based on what they all want, instead of focusing on their needs, and taking whatever is left over from their income and putting it into assets that will appreciate money. Robert Kiyosaki's 'Rich Dad Poor Dad' is a good book to illustrate this point. I recommend reading that to understand how most people are kept in a perpetual cycle of debt and liability, and what the cashflow quadrant means.

As you have seen above on the chart, when your family earns about $5000 after taxes, it does not leave much wiggle room for anything extra. When a problem arises, that is when loads are taken out because the income cannot cover something that was not planned for, such as a car repair, an appliance breaking, accidental damage, leisure activities, or even just eating out once a month. It is shocking to see most people ordering food four–five times a week and spending $50-80 a night because their grocery budget is not carefully planned. Vegetables are made to be expensive to purchase, and most people have no clue how to prepare them, leaving them to spoil in the fridge to eventually be discarded. Frozen prepared meals and ready-to-eat products at grocery stores become the most sought-after products because of the lack of interest and time by a household to be able to make a proper meal at home.

The aim with your wants is for them to fit into your needs. If you need a car, you do not need to have a car that blows your

101

budget. You need a car that you can afford, and that will not kill your finances. If you earn a total of $5000 after taxes, the most you should be spending on your car (this includes insurance AND payments) is 10 percent of your monthly income. Do you make $5000? You spend $500. If insurance costs you over $200, the car should cost you less than $300. Remember, salespersons will not care what your budget is. They will aim to push your limits because their commission depends on you making that purchase. Do you really think they have your best interest in mind? Here is a good test to see if the salesperson really gives a s**t about what you have explained to them. They will show you cars in your budget! It is a crazy thought! If you say you cannot afford more than $300 a month, and they show you a car that starts at $400, just walk away. It is no longer in your best interest to shop there. When a salesperson approaches and asks, "What are you looking for?" It should be followed up instantly with "What price are we able to work with?" They know exactly what their inventory costs. If you are shown a product out of your range, walk away. I cannot stress that enough... WALK. AWAY.

When you get a glimpse of your monthly expenditures, you will quickly understand what a necessity is and what is a luxury. If you cannot see the difference between the two, there is a larger problem in the background that needs to be addressed. Seek wise counsel in the form of a financial advisor, a financial planning course, or even someone you know who is good with money. Any advice that you seek from a reliable source will be beneficial. As I mentioned earlier, the world is your classroom. It is up to you to have the humility to remain a student and learn everything you can to have a joyful and prosperous life.

The Big Financial Decisions You Do Not Learn About

Buying a Home and getting a Mortgage

Unless you inherit $500,000, it is unlikely you can outright purchase the property. You will need to apply for a mortgage. Banks make the process incredibly easy by running a background check, confirming your income, and then giving you a maximum you can borrow. There is also a lot they do not tell you, such as penalties, equity, fixed versus variable, Assets, Amortization, Principal, Capital, APR (annual percentage rate), Escrow, and Down Payment.

Forgive me, what I mean to say is that they may tell you what the terms mean, but they will never explain it to you because it is easier to get money from a sucker than from someone informed. Have you seen ads telling you that you do not need to have a 20 percent down payment because, with the leftover capital, you would be able to invest? What about the ones that say taking a 15-year term is less advantageous in the long term because if you take a 30-year term and set aside the difference in what your monthly payment would be and invest it, you would be able to retire a millionaire? Let us address these two situations first before moving on.

A Mortgage is the largest and longest debt you will ever have. How do you manage mortgage payments reasonably?

There is something called the stress test that banks use now to protect themselves from default from the client (you). 38 percent of your total gross income is the maximum you can use for a mortgage payment, and that will determine your limit for purchasing a home. The surprising thing is that most home buyers will push that limit as much as possible for some reason. I understand that the dream home at this point in your life is only $20,000 higher than your limit and sacrificing some temporary luxuries or even necessities will be tempting to be able to purchase that home, but really consider your pros and cons here.

PRO: you will own a delightful home

CON: you will struggle to make payments on other bills, will have to compromise on other necessities like transportation or food (meaning a worse vehicle to drive or more ground meats and canned vegetables), and risk going deeper into debt because trying to stay frugal over the long term is impossible for anyone to do.

There is always something that comes up every month, whether you like it or not. A simple Speeding Ticket could cause a massive rift in your household because that was a needless expense incurred that is exceedingly difficult to afford. Your personal stress test should be aimed at 38 percent of your NET income (That is after taxes and deductions are removed from your pay). Looking at this, you will understand that a $75,000/year salary is really $54,000 after deductions, meaning that you can only afford to pay $20520 a year for your mortgage, which is $1710 a month before any down payment is made.

The conversation of a down payment will come up. I also understand that there are many people on Facebook making reels about only using 5 percent down and investing the rest... the issue with this idea is your monthly payment will be significantly higher, you will need to have mortgage insurance which is an added expense that is truly not necessary if you have 20 percent down, and while taking a lump sum of money and investing it as you buy a home may seem like a good idea, it will cripple you financially in the short term. What you as a homeowner will need to understand is that the first 10 years will be the most difficult, leaving little room for splitting your money up into different areas of interest. However, after 10 years you will notice that your monthly payments are significantly lower. This will allow you to use the difference in your current payment compared to your initial payments 10 years ago and invest that monthly. As you pay off your home, the amount you invest will increase year after year.

When it comes to picking terms, it is in the bank's best interest to get you for a longer term. They will always make it sound more appealing with lower rates being locked in, or scare you with the potential of rates going up in the future and it will be a safer bet to protect yourself long term, but since the housing bubble bursting in 2007, rates have stabilized significantly compared to what we have seen in the past.

First, the down payment. Although it may seem like a promising idea to put less money down and have more left over for expenses or investments, the ugly truth is that with any down payment less than 20 percent, you will have to automatically get mortgage insurance. What this means is that the bank will charge you extra on top of your APR to protect themselves in case you default on your payments (meaning you cannot pay anymore). The bank will be covered, and you will lose everything because you are stretched out too thin. A 1 percent difference in APR is the difference between hundreds of dollars on your monthly payments. If you cannot afford a 20 percent down payment, you cannot afford the home. Plain and simple.

Now what about a 15-year term versus a 25- or 30-year term? Simply put, the shorter term will have you paying less interest overall, but the monthly payments will be higher. The longer term will have smaller payments, but you will pay more interest overall. If you can manage a 15-year term within the confines of your income, then you will have some room to play with in that situation. If you do not have any wiggle room and can only afford a mortgage on a 25-year or 30-year term, then this is just a fallacy. Imagine that your budget is $1500 a month for a mortgage payment. If you cannot get $1500 or less on the 15-year term, you should not be considering a 15-year term. If you are on the cusp of maxing out your limit of $1500 on a 30-year term, you will have no money left to invest like those ads try to dupe you into believing. An ideal situation would be that if you budget for $1500 a month on a mortgage, you spend $1300 or less, and invest the remainder. If you have payments that are on the higher end of what you can afford, finding any wiggle room will be next to impossible. This brings me to APR. The best situation is taking the smallest possible percentage in a 2–3-year timeframe. Statistically speaking, 83 percent of people break their mortgage terms before the term matures, meaning they incur a penalty to pay. This can range from the interest of three payments to the remaining interest of the entire term, depending on what you signed. There are always things that happen in your life that require moving or taking out additional equity and refinancing, but when you understand that longer terms with lower interest rates are designed that way because there is an 83 percent chance you will not finish the term and pay a penalty, you will understand that banks don't care in the slightest about your financial situation. If the APR on a 2-year term is 0.75 percent or less higher than a five-year term, it is statistically in your favor to take it, because breaking your mortgage will cost you more in the long term. I have broken two in my lifetime, one being $1400, the other being over $10,000. Banks do not care if they get paid.

This leads to the difference between a fixed rate and a variable rate. Fixed rates are typically a little bit more on the APR, but they are dangling carrots they throw at you in trying to sell you a 'safer bet' compared to getting a variable rate. Fixed means that you lock in an APR, and that is what you pay, regardless of how the economy and the markets are doing. You will have the same monthly payment for the term. A variable rate means that you will pay the base rate plus whatever hikes or drops interest rates take. Look at it this way, unless the APR is incredibly low and too good to pass up, overall, a variable rate will do better in the long term, especially since these are the ones that if broken, have a much smaller fee to pay compared to breaking a fixed rate contract. This all depends on your lender, but as a rule, this is what the difference between the two is.

Did you know that banks are not your only source of lending? Mortgage Brokers are an option that is exercised far less because of the stigma most people have around them. They are viewed as salesmen who work for a commission, so they will try to get the most out of you. That is true in a way, but the plan you pick has nothing to do with their commission. It is in their best interest to get you the best possible rates compared to banks BECAUSE they want to make a commission. If the bank offers 2.5 percent and the broker can do 2.9 percent as their best, why would you pick the broker? Banks will often have higher rates, but this does not mean it plays out exactly as I am explaining. It is still your duty to build the best option for you and your family. I am simply giving you the tools.

What is Escrow? To put it plainly, it is a third party that holds all documents, certificates, instruments, funds etc. until both parties meet all the conditions to move forward with the sale. It is just a unique way of saying the sale is 'pending'. The other way Escrow can be used is if you pay your mortgage company the insurance and property tax you owe on the home as well, and they disburse it. For many, this is a straightforward way to manage finances and it has no impact on the final total you pay.

The term 'Amortization' refers to the amount of principal and interest paid each month over the duration of your entire mortgage term. So, for example, it is when your loan matures and you pay off your loan, leaving you with one hundred percent ownership of that specific asset, and increased in value. Contrast this with depreciation, when you pay off a principal amount, and the value at the end is less than you started with (hence why buying a car is a liability, not an asset).

Equity is a term that means how much you own a specific asset. How much the property is potentially worth now compared to when you purchased it? For example, if you bought a house for $500,000 5 years ago, and now if you were to sell it, it is worth $600,000, you have $100,000 in equity simply by taking the current value into account compared to what you paid for it. This allows the homeowner to borrow more money while leveraging their home without selling it. Then you would need to refinance and restart the term based on borrowing more money than what you have in the property. In a booming housing market, it is a terrific way to leverage your home's value and be able to invest extra money. However, the danger with borrowing more money in a housing climate that is neutral or weak, is that if you were to potentially sell the home and make far less than expected, you could be out a lot of money. Therefore, only certain individuals understand that a home is actually a liability and not an asset. Your home will only make you money if you plan to flip in good housing markets frequently. If you plan to live in one place all your life, the home should never be considered an asset.

Car

When it comes to your vehicle purchase at a dealership, you have three options. Lease, Finance, or Buy. When it comes to purchasing your vehicle privately (most likely used), you have two options; finance or buy. Let us dive into the dealership options first.

Often when we think about getting a car, we will go to dealerships to check out new vehicles and whatever used options they have. These days dealerships created a few categories in the used vehicle vernacular. Pre-owned; which means used just looks and sounds prettier..., certified pre-owned; which means used, but with the added bonus of the dealership doing a basic check on the vehicle to make sure there are no MAJOR issues (I will explain shortly), and As-Is; which describes the vehicle in a condition that may or may not be road worthy, now checks have been done to it, and no issues are reported during the selling process. By major issues, as I stated earlier, this means the headlights work, the truck runs, nothing leaks, and basic safety is still intact. Sadly though, this also means that the quality of the vehicle has nothing to do with the rating they give it. Tires are at an 'acceptable' level meaning at least 30 percent tread left (which is not very good), no check engine lights are on (but that doesn't mean all the problems have been fixed because the OBD scanner can manually clear the problems without having to be fixed, leaving a ticking time bomb), and the vehicle is clean. It is a very basic list of things that they accomplish, and overall sell you a car that is road worthy, but under no circumstances does that mean it will be free of problems even 1 month after purchase. Often, we are told that the car loses 25 percent of its value simply by driving it off the lot, so buying a used car sounds like a better investment. Yes and no, and here is why.

Buying a used car will save you money, that's a given. The only issue is if you need to finance it. Banks give much higher interest rates than dealerships when financing through them for new cars. Often, certain car brands will have 0 percent APR, up to 7.9 percent for more expensive and desirable models (or when inflation goes into overdrive and the rates are raised 9 times in a row...). If you are a smart shopper, you will get what you need, and find the right deals to be able to take advantage of 0 percent or something similar. When you purchase a used car, it is unlikely you will get a rate lower than 6 percent. I have a perfect credit score, and the lowest any bank or financial institution was willing to go was 6.3 percent. Granted it was a European car, but I digress. Remember that often looking for a used car that is 2-4 years old, might cost you very close to the same as purchasing a brand-new vehicle. The only time it makes sense is when you have the cash to buy it outright, and then it would be advisable to find a private seller because both the seller and buyer are getting a better price for the vehicle than the dealership would offer. Remember that the car's total cost to you including insurance should not be more than 10 percent after deductions from your income. You will feel that financial burden if you overextend yourself.

Lease or Finance

Financing the vehicle makes sense if you intend on owning the car for 8+ years and will drive it more than 20,000km per year. Most problems start occurring for most cars around 200,000km. If you finance on a 5-year term, that will give you 3 years of a break from car expenses, less insurance and gas, except for regular maintenance.

Leasing is the better option if you are self-employed or part of a business because it can be written off as a business expense. Leasing is also a good option if you do not intend to drive the car more than 20,000km a year because, at the end of the contract, there is something called a buyout option. What you can do as the contract holder is sell the rights to the buyout and make some money when your term is over. This is not known by many as an option to take because most have no idea that it can even be done. Before your lease is up, you can auction off the rights to the buyout and make a few thousand dollars off a car that will no longer be yours anyway. That money would be very well suited for a down payment on another lease.

If you choose to lease the car because it fits the above criteria, there is one more benefit to this route, and that is peace of mind. It is hard to put a dollar amount on that but imagine if you do not know anything about vehicle maintenance and you worry that either mechanics or dealerships will rip you off. Leasing the vehicle brings peace of mind because it is not your vehicle to worry about, you are just renting it. Like a tenant in a rental home, it is not your responsibility to fix a pipe bursting, a furnace dying, an A/C not working, windows in need of replacement, or any appliances calling it quits. That is the responsibility of the owner, which in the vehicle's case, would be the dealership. Just be a good tenant and take care of the property that is lent to you, and you will not have any issues.

Financing has similar peace of mind, especially under warranty. The thing is, all new cars have a decent warranty of about 60,000km or 4 years, but problems do not even begin to occur until 100,000km at the very least. Manufacturers know this, and that is why they offer free warranties. If you plan to commute to work or take long trips, this is your best option because if you lease the vehicle, you will pay extra fees for going over the allowed KM limit. If you can always afford 10 percent of your income going to car payments for all eternity, get peace of mind. If you are more in the ballpark of paying off and being debt-free, finance and run it into the ground. Drive it if possible until repairs outweigh the value of the vehicle.

Loans and Credit

What drives the desire to borrow money? In a word, Greed. In a few more words, Envy, Lust, Vanity, Desperation. It may seem harsh, but the fact of the matter is that unless you are in business, a family struggling with massive debt is a family that did not plan and took priority of their wants instead of their needs. The desire they had to buy a nicer car than they could afford, buy a house that was slightly out of their price range, or purchase a few frivolities throughout the year like a new TV when the older one was working just fine, or new appliances because there was a desire to want a new shiny piece of hardware. There is nothing wrong with wanting these things, the issue is wanting them to the point of sacrificing your livelihood to enjoy temporary gratification. That new TV will not feel as good in a year after owning it. Those new appliances will not cook or cool food in a better manner (no matter how well it is advertised unless tens of thousands were spent), they will be a constant reminder of mistakes made. Certain situations like needing a new furnace, water heater, roof, appliance when it breaks down, or even a car is perfectly reasonable when there is a justifiable need for it, and the want does not get in the way. Inevitably, everyone will have a type of debt at one point or another in their lives, so it is best to give some advice on how to manage it rather than make you feel bad about it.

Identify what is a necessity and what is a luxury. When it comes to going into debt, many will buy things they want instead of the things that are needed in the long term. Let us say this is a pointless conversation because I am talking about prevention, not the cure. How do you get out of the hole you made? It may seem difficult and stressful but take it one step at a time.

Create a budget first identifying your monthly income and expenses.

Consolidate your debt. Collaborating with a financial advisor will help in this aspect, but so will collaborating with the people who specialize in debt consolidation. They will pay off all your loans and credits and wrap everything into one bill with a smaller interest rate that will become more manageable to pay off. When that is complete, you will be able to assess what is the reasonable amount of money a month you can address the debt with, how long it will take to pay off, and any other penalties you may incur.

Mindset Revisited – Some things to think about

There was a group of kids that really liked to draw. The teachers started giving them little gold stars on their drawings. The kids liked the gold stars because, to the kids, it is an extrinsic reward. Then the teachers stopped giving the stars for the drawings. Then the kids stopped drawing. They associated that good feeling of getting a reward for doing something they enjoyed doing, but now we're programmed to only draw when they would get something for it. For people who love what they do, it is easy to do the work that is needed. Once you program those people to do what they love for money, they will never do it for love anymore. We must be careful how much we associate external rewards with things that help us focus and work hard.

If you are about to make a change in your life and it makes you uncomfortable, that is the best feeling you can have. Finally, for the first time in your life, you will be making a decision that is best for you, and not what someone has told you to do. That is when you are about to enter uncharted waters that will force you to challenge yourself to be perfect and succeed. Aim for success and to be the best because there is no sense in shocking your system to be average.

Even if you are tired, you can go to the gym. Even if you dislike a coworker, you can still speak to them in a respectful way. Even if you do not want to do any challenging work, you can push yourself to do it. Your feelings are not a choice, your behavior, and your thoughts are always a choice. Being great is not an accident, it is a choice.

The moment you put a stop to people who take advantage and disrespect you, they will begin to call you difficult, selfish, or insane. When a person can no longer manipulate you, they will find fault in your boundaries instead of their disrespect because manipulation hates boundaries.

Abraham Hicks created the seventeen-second rule. The concept is that when you think of something for 17 seconds, it snowballs another thought. If you are thinking negatively for 17 seconds about anything, that will trigger another negative thought for 17 seconds, and so on. When you think of something that makes you happy for at least 17 seconds, that will continue to snowball into positivity and brighten up your day.

An introvert loses energy from social interactions, while an extrovert gains energy. Being an introvert, you wake up with five social tokens. Each interaction you have depletes one token. After 5 interactions you do not have the energy or motivation to talk to anyone else and feel drained. An Extrovert wakes up with zero tokens and for each conversation and interaction they have they gain one. The longer the day goes on, the more energy they will have. If you are an introvert, match together with an extrovert during social interactions so they take the attention away from you, leaving your energy level intact.

You are not your habit. You are not a procrastinator; you have a habit of procrastinating. You are not an addict; you have an addiction problem. All habits have three parts, the trigger, the pattern, and the reward. For many habits, the trigger is always stress. Once stress is triggered, your pre-programmed pattern takes over. Finally, once you get a little taste of the reward you reset yourself until you feel a trigger again. You cannot stop a

115

habit by taking care of the trigger, it will never go away. What you can do is address the pattern you fall into. It is never the problem that is the problem, it is how we deal with it.

You do not know the future. The time you have left is a mystery. The time that is gone is gone and you can never get it back. You may have had some bad experiences in the past that have caused you emotional trauma, or physical challenges. That time is gone. It is in the past. To spend your time focusing on the past is to spend the only time you have left thinking about the time that is gone. Time never stops. What time we have left is all that we have, and to spend your time now thinking of what happened is making certain that the future will be shaped like your past.

Nobody is perfect. People are going to tell you that you are perfect just the way you are, you are not. You are imperfect. You always will be. However, there is an almighty God that designed you that way. If you are willing to accept that, you will have grace; and grace is a gift. Like the freedom that we can enjoy in this country, that grace was paid for by someone else's blood. Do not forget it. Do not take it for granted. Once you have the humility to accept your faults as your own, you will find forgiveness, and grace is the gift that will bring you joy. You are and will always be loved.

The human brain cannot comprehend the negative. You cannot tell the human brain not to do something. Take a skier for example. If all a skier is thinking 'Don't hit the tree, don't hit the tree' What are they watching and focusing on? they will likely hit a tree. If the skier is thinking, 'Go for the path, aim for the snow' that will be the path they will follow. If you focus on the obstacles, all you will see are obstacles. If all you focus on is the path through the trees, you will get through them. Your focus and your perspective are your choice.

There are 84,600 seconds in a day. Imagine every morning you wake up and you have $84,600 in your bank account. It doesn't matter how you spend that money; it will be replenished the following day; however, the money will not carry over. If you do not spend anything, you will still only have 84,600 for the next day. If you knew you had that much money to start the day off with, you would not want to waste it. Why waste time?

When you have been wronged and you retaliate or hold resentment, the devil wins. When you have been wronged and held in anger, the devil wins. The reason is because the experience has changed you. He is your master because he controls your emotions. He is not your enemy, he is your master because you become a slave to the emotions. Forgiveness is hard, but when you have that in your heart instead of resentment, you will be free.

If you wake up in the morning and begin to have negative thoughts, or when your day is progressing, and you catch yourself thinking "This is not my day." "I woke up on the wrong side of the bed." "Why do I feel this way?" Just stop for a second. Start going over in your mind that for which you must be grateful. This does not mean everything that you want, but everything that you have; because what you have is substantial you just have not taken inventory yet. Everything that you are is a blessing. Remember to stop and be grateful for all those things that give you peace and joy.

It is Easy to give up. It is the simplest thing to do. "I am done, I am not going to keep going… I do not care anymore." It is easy, it is very easy. What is hard is saying to yourself "Yesterday I achieved nothing and yet I worked as hard as I could. Nothing happened from that. I am going to do the same thing today, but I am going to try harder." That is the hardest thing in the world to do. To get up every day, give one hundred percent and be in the same position as yesterday. That is a real grind. It is also what builds grit and determination. Nothing lasts forever, not even the bottom you may be feeling.

There is no time for regrets. Move on because you are responsible for who you are and what you have done, and not who you think you should be. Accept yourself for what you have done for it shaped you into the person you are. All bad experiences have taught you that you do not like them and that you want to avoid them. All good experiences taught you that you want more of them. Regret nothing because there is no reason to dwell on your past when it is already gone. Focus on the present and learn from your past to improve your future.

Undisciplined boys become undisciplined men. Children these days do not have the privilege of having both parents in the home. When a father disciplines his boys, it may seem harsh to the mother at times. Mothers do not want to see their children in pain or sorrow, but fathers understand that certain situations require harsh words and actions to get the point across. Without discipline, boys will end up jobless, or in prison, or in the grave. Women, if you love the man you married, understand that he is turning those boys to be men who have boundaries, love their mothers, love their wives, and respect those around them.

Moving

How simple is it to pack up all your things and take them from one location to another? Seems simple really, however, it can become very complicated if it involves something more than just moving out from your parent's basement.

When you first begin living on your own, you begin to collect things you would not be bothered with when living at your parent's house. Things like furniture, bedding, towels, cookware, dinnerware, books, cleaning supplies and equipment, decorations, files, collectables, entertainment, lawn care tools, and every other item you picked up over the years. Personally, I can fill up a forty-foot container with all of my crap and still run out of room.

With all of this in mind, there are several conditions you should consider when moving from one location to the next.

1. Packing time. You would be surprised to learn how many boxes you need when the time comes, and you will also be surprised that you need to be mindful of how heavy each box you make is. Books are heavy. The cookware is heavy. Plates and decorations are fragile. Plan so that you have the time and money to properly pack everything, label it, and organize the boxes in such a way that you will easily be able to find what you have packed. It may not seem important or even a waste of time, but the most effective way to label your boxes is to put large numbers on them and just label fragile if it is so. Take a notepad and list out all the items

you packed in that specific number. This is also great when it comes time to unpack or move the boxes to the appropriate rooms when you move to your new place because you will already know where to place everything and you will not have any surprises. If you are not as old school as me, itemize the list with your phone or tablet.

2. Moving Day Costs. This includes the cost of the movers (if you choose to use them), van/truck rentals, hiring help (or having some good friends that show up on time so you can pay with food and drinks), and fuel. Personally, hiring movers may be a bit more expensive than getting a truck and doing it all yourself, but you would be surprised at how much of a minor difference the final cost actually is, not to mention you being exhausted packing and unpacking the truck, then returning it once you finish. Renting a truck and doing it all myself or with some friends was only about $100 cheaper than hiring pros.

3. Lawyers. You will need to get the keys to your new place the day you are moving. Another added stressor is when you are trying to do everything yourself. Before that happens though, be sure you find a good lawyer who is reasonable in their price and recommended by others. Look for customer service comments and reliability. Nothing is worse than trying to get ahold of your lawyer and they do not have the urgency to reply to you in an appropriate time frame.

4. Cleaning. Do not be a dick and leave a messy/dirty house for the next occupant. That is disgusting and rude. I cannot tell you how many times I moved into a new home and the fridge needed to be cleaned, or the carpet needed a cleaning, or even the bathroom fans were covered in dust. If you don't want to do this, then hire a professional. I personally make it a condition of purchase from now on, and if it is not fulfilled, I send the lawyer the bill and

they forward it to the previous owner. Put the previous owner on the hook to leave you a welcoming and habitable home. The last thing you want to do after a long day of moving is cleaning before you can even take a shower and sleep.

5. Garbage. This may not be as big a deal as you think, but there will be trash to get rid of after the house is empty, and it is very unlikely you will bring it with you to dump at your new residence. Unbelievably, I asked my realtor to take care of this for me after I moved (especially if I moved out a few weeks before the new occupants arrived). Simply prepare all the trash in one neat and organized pile, and request that they just move it to the curb the day before your specific garbage day pick up. If this feels like a strange request, talk to them about it when you are negotiating a commission.

6. Personal Inspection. When you are about to leave your residence, do a rundown from top to bottom to make sure all faucets, appliances, and lights are working. You would be surprised what you can be on the hook for within the first 48 hours. Do a quick video walking through the entire place showing that you are leaving everything in good condition. The same goes for when you arrive at your new place. Before any possession enters the premises, walk through the house testing everything. If you find any items that do not work, send the information to your realtor and your lawyer for consideration and potential reimbursement. Also, if you buy a home and the appliances are included and not 'as is,' that means they are in working condition. If you discover that they do not work properly or are faulty, it is the previous owner who is on the hook to replace them. This happened with my mom when she moved. Never used the dryer (preferred to hang dry clothes) and did not write 'as is' in the ad, she was on the hook to either fix or replace the appliance.

7. Inspections with Inspector/Contractor. Hiring an inspector is wonderful and all, however, it is not as effective as hiring a licensed contractor for a few hours. They may not give you a fully detailed report on the property, but they have a much better idea of how functional the house needs to be and will look at everything. Inspectors have a variety of services, but the issue is that they give you a report of what they saw. They will not think to look at the breaker panel to see if it is overloaded, if the water heater is in decent shape if the HVAC components of the home are in good shape/how much life left they have. Sure, some might, but it is very difficult to know which will be more reliable. I can look at the windows, door, roof, foundation, and visible structural components too, the issue is finding the problems you do not know to look for. That is why I want to spend good money on an inspector who is much more meticulous.

Some things to consider. If you are moving across the country or to a different country, try to get rid of as much as possible before your move. This is also when you need to consider a container to move instead of a truck or movers. You are looking at a cost of thousands. Containers can range from $4000-$5500 moving cross country. A Truck will be the daily cost, plus the fuel you will need, plus the mileage you put on the truck. It can be very pricey and exhausting by comparison. Moving companies that go cross-country can be a good idea, but also a dangerous option. When they quote you, they will typically give you a price for the size of the truck you will need to fill. When they show up, they will charge you per item you place on the truck. The quote can range from $2500-$4000; however, the bill can come out to $6000+ simply because they changed the terms of your move, and they would be holding your items hostage unless you pay them in full. When looking for a moving company, reputation is everything. Save all your conversations and ask as many questions upfront as you can. Personally, I prefer going the container route because you work on your timeline, the container is sealed and nothing inside is ever touched until you open it again, and if your move schedule alters, it doubles as a storage container that you can pay a small monthly fee for the company to hold until you are ready to claim it. Always do your due diligence and find what works best for you.

Insurance Ins and Outs

"The only thing worse than not having insurance is having the wrong insurance." – Unknown

Life Insurance

Life insurance is a financial tool that provides a tax-free benefit to designated beneficiaries in the event of the policyholder's death. Life insurance can provide financial security to loved ones left behind, covering the costs of burial and other end-of-life expenses, paying off debts or mortgages, and providing income replacement for dependents. In this analysis, we will discuss the basics of life insurance, including how to obtain it, when to apply, how to borrow from it, and any potential pitfalls to be aware of.

How to Attain Life Insurance

The first step in obtaining life insurance is to determine your coverage needs. This will depend on your personal circumstances, such as your age, income, assets, debts, and dependents. An insurance agent or financial planner can help you evaluate your needs and choose the appropriate type and amount of coverage.

The two main types of life insurance are term life and permanent life insurance. Term life insurance provides coverage for a set period of time, usually 10, 20, or 30 years, and is often the most affordable option. Permanent life insurance, on the other hand, provides coverage for life and includes a savings component called cash value. Permanent life insurance can be significantly more expensive than term life insurance, but it may be appropriate for certain individuals with more complex financial situations.

Once you have determined your coverage needs and the type of insurance you want, the next step is to apply for coverage. This typically involves completing a health questionnaire and undergoing a medical exam, which may include blood work and other tests. The insurance company will use this information to determine your premium, which is the amount you will pay for coverage. If you have any pre-existing health conditions, your premium may be higher, or you may be denied coverage altogether.

Best Time to Apply for Life Insurance

The best time to apply for life insurance is when you are young and healthy, as this will typically result in lower premiums. According to a study by the Life Insurance and Market Research Association (LIMRA), the average life insurance premium for a 35-year-old non-smoking male is about $250 per year for a $250,000 policy, while the average premium for a 50-year-old non-smoking male is about $950 per year for the same policy. This demonstrates that waiting to purchase life insurance can significantly increase the cost of coverage.

How to Borrow Money from Life Insurance

One of the unique features of permanent life insurance is the ability to borrow money from the policy's cash value. This can provide a source of tax-free loans for a variety of purposes, such as paying for college, purchasing a home, or starting a business. To borrow money from a life insurance policy, the policyholder must first build up enough cash value, which can take several years.

The process of borrowing from a life insurance policy is simple. The policyholder can request a loan from the insurance company, and the loan will be taken from the policy's cash value. The policyholder will then need to repay the loan with interest, typically at a fixed rate. Failure to repay the loan can result in a reduction of the death benefit or even the cancellation of the policy.

Pitfalls to Watch Out for as a New Client

While life insurance can provide valuable financial protection, there are some potential pitfalls that new clients should be aware of. One of the biggest is purchasing too little coverage, which can leave loved ones without the financial resources they need in the event of the policyholder's death. A study by LIMRA found that 30 percent of households in the United States do not have any life insurance coverage, and those that do have coverage often have less than they need.

Another pitfall to watch out for is purchasing too much coverage. While it may seem like a good idea to have as much coverage as possible, the cost of higher premiums can quickly add up and eat into your budget. It is important to find the right balance of coverage and affordability.

Another potential pitfall is not reviewing and updating your policy regularly. As your life circumstances change, such as getting married, having children, or changing jobs, your coverage needs may also change. Failing to review and update your policy can result in inadequate coverage or higher premiums than necessary.

Additionally, it is important to be honest and accurate when completing your application and health questionnaire. Failing to disclose pre-existing health conditions or lifestyle factors, such as smoking, can result in a denial of coverage or the cancellation of the policy. It is important to remember that the insurance company will investigate any claims made under the policy, and any misrepresentations or omissions can have serious consequences.

Another potential pitfall is purchasing insurance from an unreliable or unscrupulous provider. It is important to research the insurance company and agent or broker before purchasing coverage, checking for complaints or negative reviews. Additionally, be wary of agents or brokers who pressure you to purchase coverage or make promises that seem too good to be true.

Finally, it is important to understand the terms and conditions of your policy, including any limitations or exclusions. For example, many life insurance policies have a suicide clause that excludes coverage for suicide within the first few years of the policy. Additionally, some policies may have exclusions for certain types of activities, such as extreme sports or hazardous occupations. Understanding these limitations and exclusions can help you avoid surprises down the road.

The length of time that a policyholder must wait before being able to borrow against the cash value of their life insurance policy can vary depending on the insurance provider and the specific policy. Some policies may allow policyholders to borrow against the cash value immediately, while others may require a waiting period of several years. In general, the waiting period is typically between two and five years. During this waiting period, the cash value of the policy will accumulate and grow through interest and other investment returns. Once the waiting period has passed, policyholders may be able to borrow against the cash value up to a certain limit, which is typically a percentage of the total cash value of the policy.

It is important to note that borrowing against the cash value of a life insurance policy can have potential consequences, such as reducing the death benefit or causing the policy to lapse if the loan and interest are not repaid. Therefore, it is important to carefully consider the pros and cons of borrowing against the cash value before making the decision to do so.

When a policyholder borrows against the cash value of their life insurance policy, the interest on the loan is typically accumulated and added to the outstanding loan balance on a regular basis. The interest rate on the loan is typically set by the insurance company and may be fixed or variable. The policyholder is responsible for repaying the loan and interest in a timely manner. If the policyholder does not repay the loan and interest, the outstanding balance will be deducted from the death benefit or may cause the policy to lapse. If the policyholder is unable to repay the loan and interest, the insurance provider may offer the option of paying the interest only, leaving the outstanding loan balance to be repaid later. However, this can reduce the overall value of the policy and can have a significant impact on the death benefit paid out to beneficiaries.

Additionally, if the loan and interest are not repaid and the outstanding balance exceeds the cash value of the policy, the policy may lapse, which means that the policyholder will no longer have life insurance coverage. In general, most insurance providers will allow policyholders to borrow up to a certain percentage of the total cash value of the policy, typically ranging from 50 percent to 90 percent of the cash value. However, it is important to keep in mind that the outstanding loan balance will accrue interest over time, which can impact the overall value of the policy.

A general rule of thumb is to keep the outstanding loan balance to no more than 10-20 percent of the total cash value of the policy, to minimize the potential negative impact on the policy's overall value. However, this may vary depending on the individual's financial goals and circumstances.

Carefully consider the potential consequences and make sure that the loan and interest are repaid in a timely manner to avoid any negative impact on the overall value of the policy. Additionally, it is important to consult with a financial advisor or insurance professional to determine the best course of action based on your individual needs and circumstances.

Overall, borrowing against the cash value of a life insurance policy can be a useful financial tool in certain situations. However, it is important to carefully consider the potential consequences and make sure that the loan and interest are repaid in a timely manner to avoid any negative impact on the overall value of the policy.

Insurance – Car and Home

Car insurance and home insurance are two of the most important types of insurance that people typically have. They provide coverage in case of unexpected events that can cause financial loss and protect people's investments in their vehicles and homes. Here are some of the benefits and needs of car and home insurance:

Benefits and needs of Car Insurance:

1. Financial protection: Car insurance provides financial protection against damages and injuries that result from an accident. It covers the cost of repairing or replacing your vehicle, and it can also help pay for medical bills if you or anyone else is injured.
2. Legal protection: Car insurance is also legally required in most states. It can protect you from legal liabilities if you are responsible for an accident that causes damage or injury to others.
3. Peace of mind: Having car insurance can give you peace of mind, knowing that you are protected in case of an accident. You can drive with confidence and focus on enjoying the road.
4. Legal requirement: As mentioned above, car insurance is a legal requirement in most states. Driving without insurance can result in hefty fines and legal consequences.
5. Protection against financial loss: Cars are expensive investments, and accidents can cause significant financial loss. Car insurance helps protect your investment and provides financial protection.
6. Protection against liability: If you cause an accident that results in damage or injury to others, you can be held liable for the damages. Car insurance can protect you from these potential legal and financial liabilities.

Benefits and Needs of Home Insurance:

1. Protection against damage: Home insurance provides protection

against unexpected damages caused by natural disasters, fires, theft, and other perils. It covers the cost of repairing or rebuilding your home, and it can also provide coverage for personal belongings.

2. Liability protection: Home insurance can also provide liability protection if someone is injured on your property or if you are responsible for damage to someone else's property.

3. Peace of mind: Just like car insurance, home insurance can provide peace of mind. You can rest assured that your investment is protected, and you have coverage in case of unexpected events.

4. Protection against financial loss: Your home is likely one of the most significant investments you will ever make. Home insurance provides protection against financial loss caused by damage or destruction of your property.

5. Protection against liability: Home insurance can also protect you from legal and financial liability if someone is injured on your property or if you are responsible for damage to someone else's property.

6. Lender requirement: If you have a mortgage, your lender will likely require you to have home insurance. Lenders want to ensure that their investment in your property is protected.

Car insurance is attained in several ways. You can go directly to the underwriter in a particular company (such as State Farm, Co-Operators, Intact to name a few) and get quotes from the companies directly. The other method is to find an insurance broker. They take it upon themselves to get you the best rates by pitting many companies at their disposal against each other to see which rates will best suit your needs and pocketbook. The broker does not attain a commission based on the value of your plan; they get a commission based on making the sale. Most brokers I would say are there to find what you need more than a large company would if you contact them directly.

Keep in mind all of the information you need to provide in order to get the best possible rates: Age, sex (sadly this is still a criterion), driving experience, whether you took a driving course, any demerits, age of your vehicle, driving history (if you had previous accidents or claims), voluntary monitoring (if you have a chip installed in your vehicle to track your driving habits), proximity from home to work, and general usage of the vehicle in question (meaning work-related or leisure). You will attain the best quotes if your work is 15 km or less from your home, if you are female, if you have driven for 7 years or more, if you have a clean driving history, if your vehicle is relatively new (parts are easier to replace the newer your car is. Older models cost more to insure because parts are harder to come by, especially if the make and model are not common), and if you are willing to be monitored on your driving habits. If anything outside of perfect, expect rates to be higher. Shop around often. Do not feel like you need to be loyal to a specific company. If the rates that are being provided are unreasonable or if you can find better, go for it. Nothing is holding you down to a specific company.

For Home insurance, different criteria apply. Things to take into consideration for the best possible rates on home insurance include Location (homes in crime-ridden neighborhoods or those prone to natural disasters will be much higher to insure), home value, age of the home (the newer the cheaper the insurance as fewer items will have to be maintained), type of construction (fire resistant materials will be cheaper to insure than wooden frames), safety features (alarms, deadbolts, smoke and CO_2 detectors for example), previous claims history on the home, homeowners credit score, occupancy (is it for you or for a renter), and finally the size of the liability coverage. If you have $60,000 worth of valuables in your home, that will cost less to insure than if you have $200,000 worth of valuables for example.

From personal experience, it is wise to call multiple companies and brokers. When calling a broker, ask them which companies they have a relationship with. It will save a lot of time having to spend 30 minutes attaining a quote from a company you have previously dealt with. If the quote seems unreasonable, that's because it most often is. The job of insurance is to take as much from you as possible. Looking in your house and considering what you want to protect in case of theft or damage; besides appliances, furniture, electronics, and jewelry, there really is not much that you need to insure. No robber will steal your clothes... they will aim for the high-ticket item they can sell quickly. Avoid having a lot of that in your home and avoid advertising it to your community. You would be surprised that most burglars come from within your neighborhood.

So, all of that information is good and wonderful. The real problem lies in getting the insurer to actually fulfill their obligations and cough up the money when you need it. With a vehicle, it is much more straightforward than with a home.

If your car gets damaged and you are not at fault, you need to obtain the license and insurance information of the other party involved. A police officer needs to assess the damage and determine the cause of the damage (if not it will be far more difficult to prove who is at fault and who will have to pay their deductible). Call your insurance company with the details, and they will guide you to a mechanic who will assess the damage and provide the insurance company with a quote. If you are at fault, you will need to pay your deductible before the insurance company provides their service, but if you are not at fault, the deductible will be covered by the other party (most likely), and you will just have to deal with the inconvenience.

As for home insurance, deductibles are typically much higher. For a vehicle, your average would be about $500 per claim, whereas for your home it can be anywhere from $2000 to $5000 before any work even gets fixed. It becomes hard to prove a no-fault accident that happens at home especially if it is a fire or water damage unless weather is a factor. Keep in consideration that if the repair will cost the price of your deductible or less, you will be better off eating that cost and not claiming it through insurance. If the damage is significant and will cost more than the price of the deductible, it would be wise to get your insurance involved, mainly because they have specific contractors they hire to make sure the repair work is done correctly. If you have no experience dealing with contractors, this will be a wise path to follow.

If you are a landlord, there is a whole other bag of cats that I do not want to let loose, unfortunately. If you are in that position where you own multiple properties, likely you will already possess the knowledge of what to do.

Investing – In the Market

"We don't have to be smarter than the rest, we just have to be more disciplined than the rest." – Warren Buffett

"The Stock Market is designed to transfer money from the active to the patient." – Warren Buffett

"Wide diversification is only required when investors do not understand what they are doing." – Warren Buffett

Why so many Buffett quotes? Because he makes great points.

Ask yourself something. Why are all the wealthiest men and women on the planet old? Don't get offended… simply look at the ratio of successful young entrepreneurs vs. older investors. Wisdom comes with experience and age. Youth brings the motivation and focus for success.

You will never have a wealthy person like Warren Buffett making hasty or poor decisions in his youth. All the wealth and success come in time, and patience is the greatest strength you can achieve.

If you want to be a successful trader, this is a school that you need to graduate from that does not exist. There are many people and companies out there peddling their ideas and get-rich-quick strategies, but this takes just as much time to learn and master as any other profession. The biggest difference between a Trade and a Trader is simple. One is significantly more physical, while the other is significantly more emotional.

What is the biggest problem for many individuals? They have their emotions dictate their state of mind. While working at any job, you will notice that you are physically tired after the day is over. The higher positions you get, the physical strain turns into an emotional strain and becomes harder to deal with. We know that acupuncture, massages, physiotherapy, or a Spa Day helps treat physical strain and helps with the recovery time of physical stress. Most of us have no idea how to handle emotional stress and what outlets we have at our disposal to assist with managing the turmoil going on in our minds.

Trading is a very emotional and mental game. If you are impulsive, quick-tempered, affected tremendously by good or unwelcome news, or looking for pleasures that will make you temporarily happy, then I would strongly advise that you fix your mindset before diving into the financial marketplace.

Look at the greatest investor of all time, Warren Buffett. All his moves are carefully thought out and analyzed. He is patient and disciplined. There is a lot of information he absorbs before making a financial decision. That is why you often hear him say things like the quotes above that target patience and discipline. If you lack discipline, it will be incredibly difficult to learn patience.

There are multiple things you go through in life to help teach you discipline. But before I get into it, let us dissect what it means to have discipline.

Discipline is action or inaction that is regulated to be in accordance with a particular system of governance. Discipline is commonly applied to regulating human and animal behavior in the society or environment it belongs. It is training your brain to accept a specific set of rules through punishment. This is not the context in which I am applying the word. In this instance, Discipline is the ability to control yourself through demanding situations. (Both are acceptable definitions if you want to fact-check).

Applying discipline in the marketplace will give you control over your emotions and help you get a clear focus and understanding on your ultimate goal, profit.

When making a trade for the first time, the first emotion that goes through us is anxiety, then doubt, then fear, then regret. Especially if you make a losing trade. If you start off by making a winning trade, you gain a false sense of confidence, allowing your emotions to make riskier decisions for a potential gain, however much of the time this is met with frustration when a loss occurs.

I recommend learning and applying these skill sets:

Learn to control emotions

Patience when making trade decisions (Based on information not emotion)

Read books on mindset

Read about how to interpret charts

Understand who controls the market and the role you play

Find a broker that is regulated

ONLY use a live account (real money) when you have successfully traded on a demo (Fake or paper money) for consecutive months.

Lastly, having an accountability partner really helps in the long term. Someone who you can share experiences with and who can help you when you feel defeated. Create a trading plan and stick to that plan. Too often people wind up winning trades outside of their rules and feel compelled to break them more often. Remember, if you win outside of the rules you set, it's dumb luck. There is a reason you created rules for yourself. Follow them.

Investing in your future – Marriage and Children

"Love, whether newly born or aroused from a deathlike slumber, must always create sunshine, filling the heart so full of radiance, this it overflows upon the outward world." –
Nathaniel Hawthorne

"Marriage is like life - it is a field of battle, not a bed of roses." – Robert Louis Stevenson

"The happiness of a married life depends upon small sacrifices with readiness and cheerfulness." – Samuel Johnson

When you think to yourself "Nobody is stupid enough to do THAT," understand that there are many people who are. Children have the mind of a sponge. They will remember the uncanny things that they see and hear and will surprise you when they start to imitate your behavior. Speaking specifically to the men since it is easier for me to relate (What a shocker!) I want you to understand something important. The way you behave in the house will be imitated by your boys primarily. Daughters are much less likely to imitate you, but they will learn what to expect from a man. The daughters will have a subconscious attraction for men who are like you, and that means the way you act towards her and your wife and the way you speak to those closest to you and your friends.

Referring to the previous points made under the 'Religion,

Politics, and much-needed faith' earlier in the book, I ramble on about the importance of your belief system and your moral understanding of the world. If you do not or if you agree with me politically, there are several truths to understand from all of this. The first fundamental principle of marriage and having a family is common core values. Both of you must agree on the blueprint before you build the home.

I want to provide 2 analogies regarding starting a life together. A relationship between two people who plan on starting a life together is like a ship setting sail on a long and unpredictable voyage. Just as a ship needs a solid foundation to withstand rough seas and changing weather conditions, a relationship needs strong values, morals, and goals to navigate the journey. Imagine 2 people who board the ship who are both qualified to direct a course and have a different destination in mind. They are wise and knowledgeable in their own respect, but cannot agree on the destination, much less the route to take. If the goals and values are not aligned, the journey will be wrought with conflict and possible disaster. It would be like 2 captains fighting over the wheel. On the other hand, if both people share common values, morals, and goals, the journey will be smoother, and they will be able to work together to overcome challenges they may face. Having a disagreement is part and parcel of a relationship, however, the ultimate goal is to remind each other of the destination and continue navigating in the right direction.

When the destination is agreed upon and it is within reach, another task is brought up, and that is building the foundation of a married relationship. Like building a home, you need the right blueprints to meet your needs. When 2 people plan to spend their lives together, it is essential that they share the same values, morals, and goals.

Just like building a house, starting a life together requires preparation, planning, teamwork, and a common blueprint. The blueprint provides a common starting point that both of you can agree on, and the construction process is like having the foundation put in place. Without the correct blueprints, the home could be built incorrectly, leading to problems later in construction. Conversely, without being able to agree on what and how to build, the project has a very high probability of failure.

Having the right blueprint means both partners know and understand what they want the final product to look like and working together on that goal is the time you need to put into constructing the home properly. You do not need a toilet in your kitchen... trust me. When you share the work and your plans align, your home will have a strong foundation, there will not be any wasted space, and the home will flow beautifully. This is a necessity before bringing children into your lives.

When it comes to raising children, having shared values, morals, and goals is incredibly important. Here's why:

Children are highly observant and impressionable, and they learn from the behavior of those around them, especially their parents. If parents have different values, morals, or goals, it can create confusion and conflict for the child. For example, if one parent values honesty and integrity, while the other parent values success at all costs, the child may struggle with conflicting messages about what's important. When parents have shared values, morals, and goals, it provides a clear and consistent message for the child. When parents are on the same page, they can provide a united front in parenting, which creates a sense of stability and security for the child.

When values, morals, and goals are aligned, parents are

more likely to work together to create a positive and supportive environment for their children. For example, if both parents value education, they are more likely to prioritize their child's academic success and work together to support their learning. If both parents value empathy and kindness, they are more likely to model and teach these traits to their children. This is not to say one is more important than the other, that comes down to the two of you.

Having shared values, morals, and goals can help parents make important decisions about how to raise their children. For example, if both parents value independence and autonomy, they may choose to give their children more freedom and responsibility as they grow older. If both parents value family time, they may choose to prioritize spending quality time together over other activities.

The Blueprint for a stable and successful Life – for Men

"Success is not final; failure is not fatal: it is the courage to continue that count." – *Winston Churchill*

"To be yourself in a world that is constantly trying to make you something else is the greatest accomplishment." – *Ralph Waldo Emerson*

I do not intend to be controversial, but it is unavoidable. 4 simple things you need to consider in order to have a head start on your life. Graduate High School. Get a job. Get Married. Have Children. Crazy right! Let's dive into it.

Former Secretary of State Condoleezza Rice has spoken about the importance of graduating high school, getting a job, and only having kids within a married environment as key factors for driving success. She has mentioned this idea in several speeches and interviews, including a speech at the 2012 Republican National Convention where she said, "We need to have high standards for our students, and we need to have high expectations for our teachers. And we need to have high expectations for our parents. Our kids can't all aspire to be LeBron or Beyoncé. But they can all aspire to be like those people who inspire us. So, we need to provide role models for them. We need to encourage them to finish high school. We need to encourage them to stay away from teenage pregnancy. And we need to encourage them to stay in the workforce."

There are several reasons why it is important to graduate high school. A high school diploma is often the minimum requirement for many jobs. Without a diploma, job options are limited. There is a potential to make higher living wages if you graduate. Studies have shown that individuals who have a diploma often earn more than those without one, and it has a significant impact on an individual's lifetime earnings and financial stability. High School is also important for personal development. Sadly, due to bad policies during COVID-19, many students in high school who were in grades 11 and 12 did not get to fully experience their remaining school years. Overall, students have a chance to explore their interests, develop their skills, and learn about the world around them. Graduating can also provide a sense of accomplishment and confidence.

What we as a society struggle with most is the alienation and belittlement of young men. Since I am a man myself, I will focus on that target audience for the next little bit. Young men, particularly those who are graduating high school do not have much guidance as to what to do with their lives after that milestone is achieved. The most important thing for them is to get into the workforce and start developing skills that will nurture their interests and also provide them with stability and purpose. Some positive aspects of getting young men out of the house and working a full-time job are:

Financial independence, Development of work ethic, Career advancement, and positive social interaction. Having a job allows young men to earn their own income and become financially independent. This can give them a sense of responsibility and self-worth, as well as provide them with the means to support themselves and their families. A job can teach young men the value of hard work and responsibility. They can learn important skills, such as time management, communication, and problem-solving, that can benefit them in future jobs and in other areas of life.

By starting to work at a young age, men can begin building a career path and gaining experience that can lead to better job opportunities and higher pay in the future. This can also help them build a sense of purpose and direction in their lives.

A job can provide young men with opportunities to meet new people, make friends, and develop social skills. This can be especially important for young men who may be struggling with social anxiety or who may not have a strong support network.

One of, if not the most troubling statistic of our time is that men are getting less 'manly.' Too often we hear of 'toxic masculinity' in our society, and that is crippling the new generation of men.

A study published in the Journal of Sexual Medicine in 2018, found that testosterone levels had declined by about 26 percent in American men between 1987 and 2004.

The causes are still being debated and studied by researchers; however, any reasonable deduction can attest to the changing social climate in our nations as a major factor. What driving force have we had in the last two decades that would push men to be less manly? A rise in 3rd wave feminism, negative portrayal of men in movies and TV shows, fear, and the biggest problem of all, laziness. Most men choose to work in less physically demanding jobs, and that has been a significant contributor to the decline of testosterone. A major way for men to build testosterone in their system is to be physically active. This trend is often referred to as 'The Testosterone Epidemic.'

Men benefit greatly from responsibility and guidance. Take for example a truck without a load. In adverse weather conditions, that truck will be fishtailing around the road and will not have much control. As soon as you put weight in the bed, the truck becomes more stable and can drive through rougher terrain. The bed of the truck is like the responsibilities men choose to avoid. The less responsibilities they have, the more likely they will swerve off the road. The heavier the load, the more likely they will slowly commit to the course they need to travel and arrive safely. There is so much to unpack when it comes to learning what it takes to be a man and what that should look like for all stages of our lives. I strongly recommend checking out the 'Real Faith' app by pastor Mark Driscoll, specifically in the 'Real Men'section as he provides discernment, guidance, and wisdom to many generations of men.

The final point is to get married and then have children.

OMG Greg that is so bad to say and controversial! You are a bigot, misogynist, sexist... down with the patriarchy... whatever.

Jesus says it best: "If you hold my teaching, you are really my disciples. Then you will know the truth, and the truth shall set you free." – John 8:32.

This little verse states the importance of seeking and speaking the truth to achieve personal and spiritual freedom. So, let me unpack why it is crucial to have children in a married environment.

Children need a mother AND a father, especially boys. Here are some fun statistics from single-parent households:

- Crime rate: Boys from single-parent households are more likely to be involved in criminal activity compared to boys from two-parent households. According to a study by the Heritage Foundation, children from single-parent homes are more likely to engage in criminal activity, accounting for 70 percent of youths in state-operated institutions and 85 percent of youths in prison.

- Graduation rate: Boys from single-parent households are less likely to graduate from high school compared to boys from two-parent households. According to the National Center for Education Statistics, in 2019, the graduation rate for male students from two-parent households was 91 percent, while the graduation rate for male students from single-parent households was 77 percent.

- Welfare rate: Single-parent households are more likely to receive welfare benefits compared to two-parent households. According to the US Census Bureau, in 2020, the poverty rate for families headed by single mothers was 30 percent, while the poverty rate for families headed by married couples was 6 percent.

- Abortion rate: Boys and men from single-parent households are more likely to be involved in pregnancies that end in abortion compared to boys and men from two-parent households. According to a study published in the Journal of Marriage and Family, children from single-parent households were more likely to have unintended pregnancies and more likely to have abortions.

- Men's behavior later in life: Boys from single-parent households may be more likely to experience negative outcomes later in life. According to a study by the Pew Charitable Trusts, men who grew up in single-parent households were more likely to have lower incomes, experience job instability, and be less likely to own a home compared to men who grew up in two-parent households.

- Boys from single-parent households may also experience higher rates of mental health issues. According to a study published in the Journal of Family Issues, boys from single-parent households were more likely to experience symptoms of depression and anxiety compared to boys from two-parent households.

The likelihood that men will grow up to be strong contributing members of society when they come from a single-parent home is low. Although not impossible, it is unlikely that these men will go on to do anything meaningful in their lives or positively affect those around them. For men to be successful, they need guidance. Without a father in the home, they will look for influence from men outside of the home, typically from the types that want to take advantage of young men and persuade them in the wrong ways.

When men do not learn self-control and responsibility, they end up destroying their own lives and those around them. Men who practice self-control and responsibility can achieve many things, including personal growth and success, healthy relationships, and a sense of purpose and fulfillment in life.

Self-control is the ability to regulate one's thoughts, emotions, and behavior to achieve long-term goals. Men who practice self-control are better able to resist impulsive behavior, delay gratification, and make decisions based on reason and values rather than immediate desires. This can lead to better health, increased financial stability, and higher levels of academic and career achievement.

Responsibility is the willingness to accept the consequences of one's actions and the duty to fulfill one's obligations to oneself and others. Men who take responsibility for their actions and decisions are better able to build trust and respect with others, maintain healthy relationships, and achieve their goals with integrity. This can also lead to a sense of purpose and fulfillment in life, as men who feel a sense of responsibility for their own lives are more likely to pursue activities and goals that align with their values and passions.

Men who practice self-control and responsibility can achieve a greater sense of agency and empowerment in their lives. They can take ownership of their choices and steer their lives in a direction that is meaningful and fulfilling to them.

If you choose to blame others for your faults or tribulations in life, you will never be successful, and that blame is simply denying responsibility. One of the key roles as parents is to understand that your children will do very stupid things and get into trouble, however, it is your responsibility to take that burden off them as they are still learning under your guidance. A child will never grow up perfect. They need guidance and nurturing as much as you do, the difference is that the child does not understand responsibility until you teach it to them.

Men, as sad as this is, many adversarial entities are going to stand in your way to be a successful and responsible adult who has self-control. As far as support for you, there are few and far between. Often, we are told to just figure it out, or to suck it up, shake it off, cry it out, and toughen up... but rarely guided on how to deal with the struggles of life. This is why it is your responsibility as a father to teach your children how, and your responsibility as a man to learn. Where can you find the help you need? I am so glad you asked!

I mentioned it before, but I have no problems repeating it to drive the point home.

Mark Driscoll's Real Men podcast is a great resource.

Joining a church and a men's group within it is a great start.

Reading the bible. As simple as that sounds, there is more to it. Reading the bible is great only if you understand the context. It is difficult to pick up the book and flip to Romans and dive in when you have no idea what is written, who it was written for, who it was written by, and what any of it means. Truly reading and understanding the bible is best done with someone who can provide context and help answer questions when they arise. God is the Father, and He is perfect. Jesus is the Son, and He is perfect. The best places to start reading from I to learn about the life of Jesus and understand why He did what He did. Everything else will fall into place.

Society is against you. I am for you. Many out there are also for you. Many want to help you. Many want to support you. Become a responsible man and find those sources to help you be the best version of yourself.

Teaching the next generation

How many years will it take to figure it all out so that you are wise enough to be a mentor for those younger than you? Too many. Our learning will never end, our wisdom will only be enough when we realize that it is a gift given to us, and not achieved through any selfish means. There will come a time when you realize that you are blessed, and in a good position to help others and teach others. God tasks us by giving the first fruits of what we earn to Him. That means giving God your best before you use the rest for yourself. This is the only thing He asks us to test Him with.

"Bring ye all the tithes into the storehouse, that there may be meat in mine house, and prove me now herewith, saith the Lord of hosts, if I will not open you the windows of heaven, and pour you out a blessing, that there shall not be room enough to receive it."– Malachi 3:10

Our gifts are not to be used selfishly. We are tasked to share what we have learned with those willing to accept it. This includes financial wealth just as much as wisdom, and spiritual wealth. Do not think that you will accomplish everything you set out to do throughout your life. You will likely not. Priorities throughout your life will change and certain plans you made will push you off because the importance of them dwindled over time while other priorities got moved up to the front of the line. Enjoy your life with those you love, and it will make life worth living.

As a father, my duty is to teach my children everything I

know so that they may become greater than I will ever be. It will then be their duty to teach their children. As a husband, my responsibility is to be a constant source of support, care, and dependability for my wife, until the day I die.

"I have set the Lord always before me: because he is at my right hand, I shall not be moved." - Psalm 16:8.

I will be able to meet my Lord after all this has been achieved and say without any doubt that I led a good life.

Recommended Reading:

"Your next five moves" – Patrick Bet-David
"The Problem with Christianity: Finding a Faith That Makes Sense" – Mark Driscoll
"The Magic of Thinking Big" – David J. Schwartz
"How to win friends and influence people" – Dale Carnegie
"Rich dad poor dad" – Robert Kiyosaki
"Pitch Anything" – Oren Klaff
"Woke Inc." Vivek Rameswamy
"Warren Buffett and the interpretation of financial statements" – Mary Buffett and David Clark
The Holy Bible (KJV if you like ye olde English, otherwise ESV or NKJV are just fine ;)